NOT TO BE IGNORED

young people, poverty and health

**Anne Dennehy, Lee Smith
and Paul Harker**
**with George Davey Smith
and Yoav Ben-Shlomo**

CPAG Ltd, 1-5 Bath Street, London EC1V 9PY

CPAG promotes action for the relief, directly or indirectly, of poverty among children and families with children. We work to ensure that those on low incomes get their full entitlements to welfare benefits. In our campaigning and information work we seek to improve benefits and policies for low-income families, in order to eradicate the injustice of poverty. If you are not already supporting us, please consider making a donation or ask for details of our membership schemes and publications.

Poverty Publication 95

Published by CPAG Ltd
1-5 Bath Street, London EC1V 9PY

© CPAG Ltd 1997

ISBN 0 946744 90 4

A CIP record for this book is available from the British Library.

Cover illustration by Fiona White and design by Devious Designs 0114 275 5634
Typeset by Nancy White 0171 607 4510
Printed by Progressive Printing UK Ltd 01702 520050

CONTENTS

ACKNOWLEDGEMENTS

This book would not have been produced without the help of an expert advisory group the members of which are listed below:

Dr Waqar Ahmad
Dr Karl Atkin
Dr Danny Dorling
Professor Lesley Doyal
Dr Aidan Macfarlane
Professor Jerry Morris
Dr Chris Power
Dr Richard Reading
Mr Richard Wilkinson

We would also like to thank the following who commented on drafts of sections of the book:

Dr Sue Bennett
Ms Michaela Benzeval
Ms Alice Cruttwell
Ms Susan Elizabeth
Ms Lisa Harker
Ms Deborah Lyttelton
Dr Carol Tozer

FOREWORD

The link between ill health and poor socioeconomic conditions has been firmly established. The picture is one of avoidable death, disease and disability, with the loss of life linked with higher risk of deprivation estimated to be equivalent to a major aircrash or shipwreck every day.[1] Health inequalities are an endemic characteristic of all modern industrial countries but differences between countries suggest that the extent of health inequalities in the UK is not an inevitable fact. *Not To Be Ignored* is a reminder that something can and must be done.

Child Poverty Action Group (CPAG) and the King's Fund have witnessed the same problem from different perspectives. At CPAG the unprecedented rise in inequality and poverty and, in particular, the decline in living standards of families with children,[2] has sparked concern for the health of current and future generations. The King's Fund's work on health inequalities has highlighted the impact of poverty and low income on health. Our routes to understanding the problem may be different but our conclusions are the same: poverty is a major cause of ill health.

Despite substantial research, gaps remain in the literature. Health inequalities research has almost entirely been focused on infants, young children or adults. In contrast, less attention has been paid to young people. To attempt to fill this gap, CPAG and the King's Fund decided jointly to commission research with two specific aims. First, to pull together a range of disparate material about the health and socioeconomic circumstances of young people. Secondly, and perhaps more importantly, to identify evidence about health care interventions and social policy initiatives that could improve the health and life chances of young people living in poverty. On the basis of a research grant awarded by the King's Fund, the team at Bristol's Department of Social Medicine was given the unenviable task of producing a thorough and authoritative text to an impossibly tight deadline. It is to their credit that such a comprehensive publication has resulted.

The health picture in relation to young people is a seemingly contradictory one. On the one hand, adolescence is widely perceived to be a healthy period of life and a great deal of the literature which considers physical health supports this belief. On the other hand, evidence of young people's experience of drugs and alcohol and the rise of depression and teenage suicide suggests a group of the population increasingly at risk of ill health. Most commonly, research has tended to focus on single health issues across a variety of ages, which makes interpreting research in relation to young people specifically a particularly difficult 'jigsaw puzzle' task.

Investigating the link between poverty and ill health among young people is particularly complex because of the changing nature of young people's circumstances. Income, earnings or social class can be used as a proxy for the socioeconomic circumstances of adults. But a young person may be entirely dependent on his or her parents for resources or may be fully or partly independent, reliant on their own income or benefits. For this reason, young people need to be viewed in the context of their family as well as independent young adults.

Despite such difficulties there are good reasons for paying particular attention to the health of young people. This stage of life is a crucial one in determining future health. Between the ages of 10 and 19 young people experience a critical period of transition both in terms of their health needs but also their socioeconomic status. It is a period of life which involves increasing uncertainty: changing dependency status, the learning of new, potentially health-damaging behaviours, greater geographic mobility and changing relationship with others, including professionals working in the area of health.

As the following pages reveal, there is evidence to suggest that poverty does have a detrimental impact on young people's physical and mental health. In Chapter 2, the authors identify a range of health problems in young people associated with poor socioeconomic status including: accidents, respiratory illness, depression, schizophrenia, suicide and eating disorders, sexually transmitted disease and substance abuse. The evidence appears to contest previous findings that the health inequalities among young people are minimal.[3] Indeed, the evidence suggests that the common health problems are those which can affect health in adult life.

In the face of such evidence it is vital that a strategy is developed to improve the health and life chances of young people living in poverty. Policies to reduce inequalities need to address the broad range of factors that affect people's health: their physical environment;

their social and economic circumstances; barriers to adopting a healthier lifestyle and their access to appropriate and effective health and social services.[4] Despite this, policies have tended to focus on just one aspect: unhealthy behaviours. A much broader approach is required.

The balance between health and social interventions is likely to be a critical one. The message from research is that poverty can undermine the effectiveness of health intervention strategies. Various social and economic factors have been established as being of crucial importance in determining health, including income and wealth and the physical environment (such as the adequacy of housing). Such factors are, in turn, determined by access to education and training and the availability of employment.

Young people have, to a great extent, faced the brunt of social and economic change in recent years, accompanying a growth in income inequality to a level not witnessed since the World War II. The incomes of the poorest 10 per cent of the population fell by 13 per cent between 1979 and 1993/94, while the richest 10 per cent saw a rise of 65 per cent.[5] Poverty has tripled among families with children since 1979 and children now make up a larger group of the poor than pensioners. The opportunities for young people have shrunk with the rise in unemployment and at the same time benefit restrictions have been introduced which have removed entitlement to benefits for 16 and 17 year olds except in cases of severe hardship. Some talk of a 'status zero' generation whose education, training and employment opportunities are closed and whose aspirations and hopes have deteriorated.[6]

Education and training are key experiences – both in terms of identifying and meeting health needs and in preparing young people for other aspects of life and thereby helping to determine their life opportunities. But socioeconomic support for young people starts before school age – preschool provision has been shown to have a long-lasting beneficial impact. The right start in life could prevent the need for more substantial intervention later in life. Other socio-economic initiatives which would benefit young people would form part of a wider strategy to reduce inequalities in the population as a whole. This includes addressing the income needs of families with children and young people of working age, which requires welfare to work initiatives as well as support for those out of work. In addition, changes in taxation policies would significantly reduce income inequalities. The framework of policies outlined in Chapter

4 would significantly reduce the inequalities in opportunities which young people currently face as well as benefiting others in society.

Despite the significance of social and economic interventions, it is also important that local services for health and wellbeing do not abdicate their responsibilities for tackling health inequalities and play their role in promoting social justice and equity in health. In Chapter 3 the authors show that there is limited research evidence available on the effectiveness of services for young people's health. The research which has been undertaken has tended to overlook the views of young people and has favoured quantitative data over qualitative information. There are important lessons to be learnt about the design, conduct and evaluation of research methodology in this area of work.

Much of the available evidence suggests that the lack of success which local interventions have had in reducing health inequalities among young people may be due to services not reaching young people and/or those living in poverty. A radical rethink is required concerning the appropriate setting for services (within and beyond mainstream health provision), the type of professional best equipped to provide services and style of approach. It may be the case that young people can show us the answers if we listen to them.

The health inequalities among young people will only be tackled if an integrated approach is taken, one which brings together the most effective social and economic and health interventions united by a commitment to change. In Chapter 5 various options are considered. A key challenge is identifying the process by which such an approach can be taken. A national strategy led by government is required to provide the framework. At the local level interventions must be appropriate, well resourced and responsive to socioeconomic as well as health needs. The evidence in favour of a new approach is overwhelming. We hope that this publication will contribute to a debate about the way forward. We believe that the impact of poverty on young people's health is simply an issue which is not to be ignored.

Lisa Harker, Child Poverty Action Group
Michaela Benzeval and Susan Elizabeth, The King's Fund
February 1997

NOTES

1. B Jacobson, A Smith and M Whitehead (eds), *The Nation's Health: A strategy for the 1990s*, King Edward's Hospital Fund for London, London, 1991.
2. C Oppenheim and L Harker, *Poverty: The Facts*, CPAG Ltd, 1996.
3. S Macintyre and P West, 'Lack of class variation in health in adolescence: an artefact of an occupational measure of social class?', *Social Science and Medicine*, 1991, 32(4): 395-402.
4. M Benzeval, K Judge and M Whitehead (eds), *Tackling Inequalities in Health: An Agenda for Action*, Kings Fund, 1995.
5. DSS, *Households Below Average Incomes: A Statistical Analysis, 1979–1993/94*, HMSO, 1996.
6. 'The Status Zero generation', *Daily Telegraph*, 13 October 1995.

How poverty affects the lives of young people

YOUNG PEOPLE NEED MORE

You take the space
You have for granted

    Your spacious living room
    And your well-ordered lives
    The estate in the drive outside

This is your creativity
    Your house and your work

The fact that you have
Money in your bank account
Your justified rewards

What about these young people
Standing on street corners
Answerable to everyone
But themselves?

    Where is their space
    Who is giving them their just desserts?

Is this all they deserve?
    TV
    A disused bus shelter
    Or a nostalgic trip down
    The kid's playground
    In the park
    Reprimands

And the constant
Monitoring of progress

Where do they live?
Somebody else's house

Whose money is in their pocket?
The State's or Dad's

Surely they need something more than this?

More than the constant
Reminder of their own insecurity
And their own mistakes
More than all the unspoken pressures
To be fit and be normal

To be their Dad's hero
Or their Mother's scapegoat

More than a short sharp
Rap on the knuckles
By the Law

When the boredom gets too much
And they break
OUT
Into some petty crime

Just to get a sense
Of identity

A sense that
People do care
Whether they are
Alive or Dead

After all

Isn't it just about
The worst thing
For a young mind

To be ignored

This poem was written in 1994 by Penny Wildgoose, a young person living in Dudley, in the West Midlands, who gave the poem to her local general practitioner when he was fighting to support the development of a young persons' centre on a local council estate.

INTRODUCTION

This book focuses on young people as defined by the World Health Organisation, that is, those aged between 10 and 19. However, in some instances we refer to the under 10s and to young adults in their early 20s. The primary reason for this is to fit in with the way in which data are collected. For example, figures on suicide often refer to 15–24 year olds and data on smoking trends may look at young people under 15 and those under 24 quite separately. It has therefore been necessary to be as flexible as possible in order to include young people at either end of the age group we focus on.

There are three main reasons for isolating this section of the population as the focal point of the research:

- the age range of 10–19 includes the years of transition into adulthood;
- there is a dearth of literature on the relationship between poverty and health in young people;
- the extent to which the freedom to make so-called 'healthy choices' frequently depends on freedom from poverty.

Although our focus is on young people it is impossible to ignore the environmental factors and circumstances of their families and friends as, in many cases, this appears to have a profound effect on the health and wellbeing of young people in this age range. Consequently, we touch on issues such as composition of household structure, educational and employment opportunities according to gender and ethnicity, the effect of parents' unemployment on young people's health and the assumption that young people are dependent on parents who are able (and willing) to support them during this period of their lives. These issues can all affect the living standard of young people and, therefore, have implications for their health.

Chapter 1 starts by considering the labels and stereotypes that can segregate, separate and isolate young people, and discusses the need to look at young people's interpretation and experience of poverty and how this affects their wellbeing, the essence of health. The point is made that health is a continuum and the experiences of poverty from conception through childhood have effects on young people's health;

similarly, the experiences of young people can have long-term effects on their health when they have become adults. Population trends among young people, together with trends in family structure and income are seen to have widespread ramifications and these may act against the optimism of youth in wishing to belong to and to participate fully in society. Health problems can be further compounded by advertising aimed at young people who have money and in some instances deliberately encouraging unhealthy behaviour. This section closes with consideration of young people's transition to full and independent adulthood, which is so necessary for good health.

HOW NAMES BECOME LABELS AND DESCRIPTIONS BECOME STEREOTYPES

Throughout this book we aim to highlight the problems associated with the use of populist and discriminatory language to describe young people. This language can segregate, separate and isolate different groups of young people according to ethnicity, gender and socioeconomic status. Media headlines that refer to a 'yob culture' or discuss young people from lone parent families as doomed to fail, or groups of young men according to their colour, are part of the language of exclusion.

Although we aim to avoid falling into both the trap of labelling young people and the difficulty of separating this period of life from adulthood, we do address specific problems which arise because of the way in which we, as adults, manage both society and the image of young people. When possible, reference is made to young people rather than teenagers, adolescents, boys or girls and the ways in which labelling and language can discriminate against the life chances of young people is discussed wherever relevant.

Outlined below are a few of the many assumptions, social constructions and labels used by institutions which may discriminate against and exclude young people.

THE STATE

The state:
- adopts family policies based on the nuclear family;
- forms social policy based on 'Christian' values which exclude many in our multi-cultural society;
- assumes freedom to choose without considering freedom from

poverty; and
- assumes young people are supported by 'families'.

THE MEDIA

The media:
- create and perpetuate stereotypical images of young people;
- reinforce the image of the nuclear family when population trends show reality as something quite different;
- portray young people as a homogeneous consumer group; and
- frequently present young people as not capable of making their own decisions.

EDUCATION

Education:
- appears to constrain freedom of choice and opportunity for many young people who are poor, because of the new 'market' for education;
- regards free school meals as a 'label';
- perpetuates assumptions regarding the ability of young people from non-white households and those who are not part of a nuclear family; and
- often reinforces the effect of 'self-fulfilling prophecies' on young people's academic achievement.

HEALTH SERVICES

The health services:
- frequently assume that all young people are 'healthy';
- often regard young people as 'poor communicators';
- give insufficient attention to young people who do have special health requirements/needs and treatments – the latter may in particular be affected by ethnicity and gender.

SOCIAL SERVICES

The social services:
- ignore the needs of young people who are not classified as 'in need of protection'; and
- are unable to respond to all the needs of young people in care.

By addressing these issues throughout this book, it is possible to discover ways in which these socially constructed inequalities may be overcome. The continuing debate regarding the relevance of a class analysis is not included here because class is referred to in its broadest sense, using the Registrar General's (RG) definition, as this is commonly used in data analysis and official reports. There still remain the other two key concepts, both with problematic and often subjective definitions, which are the subject of much debate – poverty and health. Perhaps the most important issue to consider here is the dynamic nature of both of these concepts: they change in time and space according to the productive capacity of society, so, wherever possible we have dealt with these issues in the context of Britain in the 1990s.

POVERTY

Although this book focuses on poverty and its relationship to ill health the detailed arguments regarding the existence, nature and measures of poverty are not an integral part of the text. These debates are expanded in more detail in other CPAG titles such as *The Growing Divide* and *Poverty: the facts*. Wherever possible we use young people's interpretation of poverty, how the experience of poverty affects their everyday lives and, most importantly, the impact it has on their sense of wellbeing. This is not a definitive text on measures, definitions and official versus non-official interpretations of poverty. Rather, the concept of poverty is explored in the context of its cause and effect relationship with the health of young people.

HEALTH

The concept of health is examined here in relation to the lives of young people. It is therefore difficult to arrive at a definition of 'health' which does not involve a lengthy debate or constrain the reality of young people's health in its socioeconomic context, which is one of the objectives of this text. So, as with the nature of poverty, wherever possible we use young people's definitions, beliefs and experiences of health and wellbeing. Where health is discussed and/ or investigated in relation to academic, professional/health and sociological data, the discussion refers back to the concept of health in young people's lives in the spirit of the 1989 UN Convention on the Rights of the Child[1] in order to:

recognise the right of the child to the enjoyment of the highest attainable standard of health and to facilities for the treatment of illness and rehabilitation of health ... to ensure that no child is deprived of his or her right of access to such health care services ... to combat disease and malnutrition ... have access to education ... the prevention of accidents ... to develop preventative health care

[Article 24]

recognise that a mentally or physically disabled child should enjoy a full and decent life ... recognise the right of the disabled child to special care ... Recognising the special needs of a disabled child ... taking into account the financial resources of the parents or others caring for the child

[Article 23]

[and to acknowledge:]

the right of every child to a standard of living adequate for the child's physical, mental, spiritual, moral and social development ... State Parties ... shall take appropriate measures to assist parents ... and shall in case of need provide material assistance and support programmes, particularly with regard to nutrition, clothing and housing

[Article 27]

Interviews and comments from the young people we cite, and those from other contemporary research, concur with the Articles referred to above and show how health is not merely the absence of illness but a sense of wellbeing and freedom: where equality enables all young people, regardless of ethnicity, creed, colour, gender or ability, to live life to the full based on the expectations and aspirations of society as a whole. This definition of health is, it may be argued, all-embracing, but the age period of 10–19 years is a complex period of transition. Not only is it associated with a series of biological changes, such as the pubertal growth spurt and development of secondary sexual characteristics, it is also a period fraught with major social change, a period which may involve the end of schooling and the start of higher or further education, leaving home, entering the labour market and, sometimes, becoming parents. The aim here is not to medicalise these natural progressions through life, but to examine the relationship between poverty and health during these major transitions. However, health is influenced by factors arising across the life course and some reference is made to peri- and postnatal influences on the health status of 10–19 year olds and how these earlier years affect health and wellbeing during mid-life and old age. It is therefore important to look at the broader social context of health and illness with reference to studies which cover mortality, morbidity, wellbeing, health-related behaviours and socioeconomic indicators.

KEY MESSAGES

Stereotypes can segregate, separate and isolate young people.

Young people's interpretation and experience of poverty is crucial, as is the impact on their sense of wellbeing.

Wellbeing is the essence of health.

WHY YOUNG PEOPLE?

There has been a tendency for children's voices, in particular, to be silent.[2]

Young people experience major changes between the ages of 10 and 19 which are a natural part of the life cycle. Health research and statistics often exclude or pay little attention to this particular age group because of the assumption that young people are 'healthy' or 'resilient'. However, over the last ten years this assumption has been challenged by a wide range of research,[3-6] which suggests that young people are as vulnerable as the rest of the population. In addition, there is a range of specific health problems, such as accidental injuries, depression, substance misuse and respiratory disorders, which are of particular significance for this age group.[7]

A number of recent studies investigating the health of young people suggest that there are only small social class differences in health during this part of the life cycle.[8, 9] The lack of marked differences reflects to a large degree the difficulty in measuring health in the absence of overt disease. However, psychological differences are much more marked. Behavioural research has found that 16 year olds from social classes IV and V have worse psychological health and are more likely to exhibit so-called 'deviant behaviour'.[10] Furthermore, measures of growth and development such as height and respiratory function do show social class differences, with children from poorer homes being shorter and having worse respiratory function. Although these may not directly cause ill health in childhood, they are important as regards health in adulthood.[3, 6, 11-15]

The transitional period from childhood to adulthood also has other implications for long-term health. For example, lack of engagement in sport and exercise in childhood may precede a lifetime of low participation in these potentially physically and psychologically protective activities.[16] Similarly, lack of socialisation during childhood can actually perpetuate notions of inevitable socioeconomic inequalities. Poverty of aspiration (which has a concomitant relationship with psychological health, low academic achievement and poor labour market position) prevails in childhood and through to adolesence, thereby affecting the individual's subsequent life trajectory.

When young people are asked about their mental, physical and psychological wellbeing, they reveal a breadth of knowledge on health matters and on how society collectively fails them, in terms of health, health-related behaviours and their aspirations. By listening to young people we may be able to learn about their experience of poverty during childhood and its potential impact on health. This is important in explaining both the successes and failures of health promotion, health education and the use of health resources aimed at young people. Research to date suggests that the latter may need to be restructured, based on the knowledge we have about the reality of young people's lives, instead of on preconceived views of adolescence, which ignore the real needs of this population.

KEY MESSAGE

Study of variations in the health of young people is vital for society.

DEMOGRAPHIC TRENDS

Between 1982 and 1992 the total number of young people in England fell by over a fifth to less than six million (see Table 1.1). At the same time, the total population rose by 3.4 per cent to just over 48 million. Thus, the proportion of young people fell from 16 per cent of the total population in 1982 to only 12 per cent in 1992. However, it seems that this trend will be reversed over the next 20 years. By the year 2012 the adolescent population will increase by 10 per cent, while the increase in the total population is forecast at less than 7 per cent.

TABLE 1.1: **Population estimates and projections, England, 1982-2012 (thousands)**

| | 1982 | 1992 | Projections | | % change | | |
			2002	2012	1982-92	1992-2002	2002-12
Total population aged 10-19 years	7,497	5,872	6,400	6,481	−21.7	9.0	1.3
Total population all ages	46,807	48,378	50,194	51,566	3.4	3.8	2.7
Population 10-19 years as % of total population all ages	16.0	12.1	12.8	12.6			

Source: OPCS for 1982 and 1992 population estimates; Government Actuary Department for 2002 and 2012 population projections; On the State of the Public Health, 1993.

The proportion of the population under 20 years of age varies by geographical region. It is highest in Northern Ireland (33 per cent) followed by Scotland (26 per cent) and England and Wales (25 per cent) (*Annual Abstract of Statistics*, 129). Males are overrepresented in this age group. In 1994, 51 per cent of those between 5 and 19 years of age were males. The comparable figure for the whole population is 48 per cent.[17]

ETHNICITY

Data on ethnicity in Great Britain come from the decennial Census (questions on ethnicity were introduced into the Census in 1991) and the Labour Force Survey, which is now produced on a quarterly basis.

In 1994, the total minority ethnic population of Great Britain was estimated at 3.2 million people, approximately 1 in 18 of the overall population.[18] Results from the Labour Force Survey indicate that the proportion, size and composition of the minority ethnic population have not changed over the last few years. Groups with origins in the Indian sub-continent (India, Pakistan and Bangladesh) account for approximately half of the minority ethnic population.[18]

Around 8.4 per cent of young people in Britain aged 10–19 are from minority ethnic groups, compared with only 5.7 per cent for the population as a whole.[18] The proportion of minority ethnic children has risen slowly, with, once again, the largest group having its origins in the Indian sub-continent. They comprise 4.7 per cent of children aged 10–19 in Great Britain. Black children in this age group make up 2.2 per cent of the population, while children in other ethnic groups comprise 1.5 per cent of the population. Higher proportions of people in non-white groups live in more deprived metropolitan areas than in other areas.[19]

TABLE 1.2: **Population of 10–14 year olds and 15–19 year olds as a percentage of their ethnic group in Great Britain, 1993–1995**

	10-14 years (%)	15-19 years (%)	10-19 years (000s)
Black-Caribbean	7	5	61
Black-African	8	5	35
Other Black (non-mixed)	15	10	20
Black (mixed)	16	10	33
Indian	9	8	148
Pakistani	13	11	130
Bangladeshi	12	12	43
Chinese	7	7	19
Other Asian (non-mixed)	7	6	22
Other (non-mixed)	7	7	18
Other (mixed)	13	10	43
All ethnic minority groups	10	8	578
White	6	6	6,325

Source: Labour Force Survey (Spring 1993 to Autumn 1995, inclusive; 11 quarters' data).[18]

Non-white ethnic groups have a much younger age distribution than the white population group (see Table 1.2). The populations of mixed ethnic origin (the Black (mixed) and Other (mixed) groups) were the youngest, followed by the Other Black, Bangladeshi, Pakistani, Black-African, Indian, Black-Caribbean and Chinese populations. All were younger in age profile than the white population.[18] Rough calculations based on retrospective data from 1986–88 Labour Force Surveys suggest that the population of mixed ethnic origin has been growing at one of the fastest rates. Bangladeshi, Pakistani and African populations were also above the average growth rate for the entire minority ethnic population.[18] The estimated median ages of Other Black and Other (mixed) groups were 12 and 16 years respectively in 1994. For the ethnic minority population as a whole, the median age is 26 years.

KEY MESSAGES

The population of young people is set to increase.

Minority ethnic groups have a younger age distribution.

MEASURES OF POVERTY

Poverty, what poverty? says Lilley

Guardian, 17 April 1996

Relative poverty is real and does indeed exclude a growing number of people from sharing in the common life of the nation. Unfortunately, in Thatcherite Britain, absolute poverty was also a reality. Manifestly, it no longer exists on a Victorian scale, but it has not been eradicated ... The Conservative Party has never sought to promote equality ... on the other hand it has seldom gone out of its way to heighten inequality.[20]

Ian Gilmour, former Government minister

Poverty in contemporary society is complex, with continuing debates regarding the appropriateness of absolute versus relative measures of poverty. In this section we aim to investigate poverty with specific reference to young people, their experience of poverty and how this affects their health status. In any discussion on poverty, it is helpful to go beyond notions of material deprivation and inequalities and consider the effect of a paucity of adequate resources which are required to satisfy certain essential minimum human needs, which will be dynamic and change over time.

Relative poverty, particularly in relation to young people and their everyday lives, may be described as the absence of such basic items as warm, adequate clothing and the ability to participate in such basic social activities as going to the cinema, swimming or taking part in school trips.[3, 21] This approach seeks to determine the number of people whose standard of living is below the minimum acceptable to society. One such definition considers people in poverty to be those who have no choice but to fall below a minimum level by lacking three or more basic necessities.[22] Such a concept of poverty is dynamic as the definition is relative to the norms, values, living conditions and amenities which are customary, or at least widely encouraged or approved of, in society.[23]

Relative poverty over the past 15 years has affected an ever-increasing proportion of the population.[24] There is no official definition of poverty or the poverty line in the United Kingdom as there is in the USA and several other countries. The most common alternative measure is the one employed by CPAG, which is 50 per cent of average income after housing costs.

As well as relative poverty it is important to consider the distribution of wealth and income across the population. More egalitarian societies have narrower differences between the most and the least affluent sections of their population. Among developed countries, income distribution rather than average wealth appears to be a more important determinant of health and life expectancy, further supporting the importance of relative rather than absolute poverty.[25] In the UK, income inequality has grown rapidly between 1979 and 1993. During this time the population with average income rose by 38 per cent in real terms while those groups on below average incomes rose by considerably less. Excluding the self-employed, the poorest one-tenth of the population in 1993–95 were actually 6 per cent worse off in real terms than the poorest 10 per cent of the population in 1979 (after housing costs) (see Figure 1.1). Income inequalities are now at their highest level since World War II and appear to be increasing at a faster rate than in any other industrialised nation.[26]

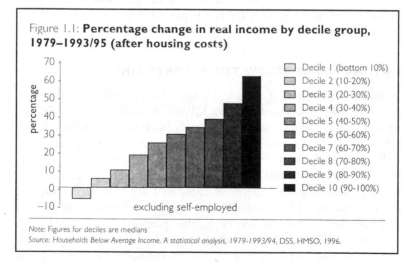

Figure 1.1: **Percentage change in real income by decile group, 1979–1993/95 (after housing costs)**

Legend:
- Decile 1 (bottom 10%)
- Decile 2 (10-20%)
- Decile 3 (20-30%)
- Decile 4 (30-40%)
- Decile 5 (40-50%)
- Decile 6 (50-60%)
- Decile 7 (60-70%)
- Decile 8 (70-80%)
- Decile 9 (80-90%)
- Decile 10 (90-100%)

excluding self-employed

Note: Figures for deciles are medians
Source: *Households Below Average Income. A statistical analysis, 1979-1993/94*, DSS, HMSO, 1996.

MEASURING POVERTY AMONG YOUNG PEOPLE

Several publications since 1990 have filled a gap in the literature on poverty and the health of children,[15,27,28,29] but none has concentrated on the age group of 10–19 that is encompassed by the World Health Organisation (WHO) definition of young people.

Measuring poverty in young people is further complicated by the paucity of data for this age group. Most data are based on family poverty because the socioeconomic status of young people is obviously dependent upon that of their families until school-leaving age. Two measures used by the CPAG were *Low Income Families* (LIF) and *Households below Average Income* (HBAI) statistics.[30] In this section, the emphasis is on the latter because, in 1988, the government stopped producing LIF due to concerns about its methodology. Other proxies for poverty included in this section are consensual poverty and unemployment rates.

Households below Average Income (HBAI) statistics are the government replacement for *Low Income Families* statistics and are now the primary source of official information about people living on a low income. CPAG uses 50 per cent of average income after housing costs as a proxy, which is in line with the poverty standard adopted by the European Commission and several international studies. A more technical description of this measure and the justification for using income after housing costs (AHC) is provided in a previous CPAG publication *Poverty: the facts.*[3]

HOW MANY ARE BELOW THE POVERTY LINE?

A growing number of people in the UK are falling below the poverty line, as defined by the CPAG definition. These figures underestimate the true extent of poverty because they exclude those who are homeless and/or living in institutions. The number of individuals with income substantially below the national average has clearly risen significantly since 1979, and children are particularly overrepresented among the poor compared with adults. As poverty grew during the 1980s and 1990s, the disparity between adults and children also increased. In 1979, the proportion of adults and dependent children who fell below the poverty line was very similar (9 per cent and 10 per cent respectively). However, the latest figures from 1993/94 show that the respective figures are now 24 per cent and 32 per cent. In 1993/94 over four million children and young people were living in poverty but in 1979 the figure was 1.4 million (see Table 1.3). Children and young people have now overtaken the elderly as the largest age group in poverty.[15] Some groups appear to be at a greater risk of experiencing poverty than others. For example 41 per cent of lone parent households are said to be 'objectively' living in poverty as are 60 per cent of households where the main earner is unemployed and seeking work.

TABLE 1.3: **Numbers and proportions of the population and children who fall below the poverty line (AHC)**

	Number of people below the poverty line (millions)	% of the population below the poverty line (millions)	Number of children below the poverty line (millions)	% of dependent children below the poverty line as % of all children
1979	5.0	9	1.4	10
1988/89	12.0	22	3.1	25
1991/92	13.9	25	4.1	32
1992/93	14.1	25	4.3	33
1993/94	13.7	24	4.2	32

Source: Government Statistical Service, 1996.[31]

UNEMPLOYMENT

The economic factor that had most impact on children in the 1980s has been the high level of unemployment, unprecedented in the post war era.[32]

Unemployment has arguably become the single most important factor related to the increase in child poverty in the UK since 1979.[33] This is because of the increasing numbers of people who are unemployed, the reduction in entitlement to benefit and the fall in the value of benefits for the unemployed in relation to earnings.

Entitlement to benefits no longer exists for most 16 and 17 year olds. Furthermore, young people aged between 18 and 25 receive less benefit than those who are over 25, and so this group of people is still relying on the resources of their parents when they leave school or carry on in further education. The true extent of unemployment among young people is hidden by government training schemes which were introduced in 1981 and by changes over time in social security regulations.[13] Figures taken from the

Labour Force Survey (June 1996) summarise the severity of the unemployment situation among young people today in the UK:

- 281,000 16–19 year olds were unemployed during the winter 1995/6.
- The unemployment rate among young males is the highest of any age group (19.6 per cent).
- Unemployment is currently only rising in the 16–19 age group (increasing at 16 per cent).
- 4 per cent of men and 5 per cent of women aged 16–19 are classed as long-term unemployed, that is, they have been out of work for over a year.

THE GEOGRAPHY OF POVERTY AND WEALTH

Since 1979, the geography of poverty and wealth has altered greatly.[34, 35] Although many of the changes do not directly affect young people, a number of them have an indirect effect through the impact these changes have had on family life. One of the prime examples of this is the increase in the unemployment rate and a rise in male inactivity which generally results in a lower standard of living for young people within households. Most of these social and economic changes have been spatially uneven in their magnitude, timing and impact upon different population sub-groups. Those who lost out are spatially concentrated in particular localities, namely large metropolitan areas and/or districts within cities.

Young people are, on the whole, not as likely to be as concentrated in inner cities areas as is popularly believed.[36] Parents' mobility is at its greatest when their children are adolescent, with many of them moving out of cities and into the suburbs and the countryside.[36] However, relatively few young people in poorer families will experience this and so, again, this group is likely to be concentrated in areas of greater poverty. The scale of segregation seems to be increasing and so there is growing concern that areas of extreme poverty may become isolated from the economic and social mainstream. Minority ethnic groups are disproportionately concentrated in London, the principal cities and other metropolitan areas, which are the areas experiencing the greatest increases in poverty between 1981 and 1991.

The main conclusions regarding the changing geography of poverty for young people are:

- Young people from poorer families and ethnic minorities are overrepresented in areas of greater poverty.
- The effect of poverty on young people from rural areas is not well documented.
- Some areas, most notably Merseyside, suffer from a combination of high degree, extent and intensity of poverty to produce particularly severe socioeconomic problems in 'concentrated poverty' areas.

YOUNG PEOPLE AND THE CHANGING NATURE OF THE FAMILY

> The highest risk of being in poverty is being a lone parent family but the largest group in poverty are couples with children. The family type with the lowest chance of being in poverty and the lowest proportion of poor households are childless couples ... the more children there are, the greater the chances of being poor.[37]

Numerical and 'official' data rarely address the complex composition of contemporary society – step-families, cohabiting parents who are not married, lone parent families, lesbian and gay households and residential care are the background for a large and growing proportion of young people. The dominance of the nuclear family is increasingly questionable. Only 20 per cent of all households in the 1991 Census consisted of an adult male, an adult female and one or more dependent children. (For a more detailed discussion about the effects of changing family structure on the lives of young people, see Atkinson and Gittins.[38, 39])

Breadline Britain, cited above,[37] illustrates how young people from lone parent families have an increased risk of experiencing poverty. Lone parenthood is both a cause and a consequence of poverty.[15] However, in absolute terms, there are more young people from two-parent families who live in poverty. The number of children in lone parent families has increased (see Table 1.4), but this is not to argue that this will necessarily result in their being poorer or having worse health.

TABLE 1.4: **Percentage of dependent children by each family type in Great Britain 1979–1994**

	Married couple with one dependent child	Married couple with two or more dependent children	Lone mother with one dependent child	Lone mother with two or more dependent children	Lone father with one dependent child	Lone father with two or more dependent children
1979	18	70	3	7	0	1
1981	18	70	3	7	1	1
1983	18	69	3	8	0	1
1985	19	69	4	7	1	1
1987	19	69	4	7	0	1
1989	18	67	4	9	1	1
1991	17	66	5	12	0	1
1993	15	65	6	12	1	1
1994	16	64	6	14	1	0

Note: Dependent children are persons under 16 (or aged 16–18 and in full-time education) in the family unit and living in the household.

Source: General Household Survey, 1994.[17]

The comparatively worsening plight of children is highlighted in Table 1.5. More couples with children fall below the poverty line compared with couples without children. The pattern is more pronounced for lone parent families, with 58 per cent falling below the poverty line compared with 22 per cent of single people and 25 per cent for all family types.

This further highlights the increase not only in the numbers of lone parents but in the proportion of lone parents on low incomes (see Table 1.5). Approximately three-quarters of the unemployed also fall in the 'below half the average income category' but this is likely to be an understatement because a significant group of young unemployed people may, sometimes against their wishes, be living in households with a wage-earning parent and so find themselves with household income above half the national average, although they have few resources themselves. Since 1979 the percentage of dependent children living with lone mothers has risen from 10 to 21 per cent.[17]

TABLE 1.5: **Percentage of individuals in different family types who fall below the poverty line (after housing costs)**

	Couple with children	Couple without children	Single adult with children	Single adult without children	All family types
1979	8	5	19	7	9
1991/92	24	12	59	22	25
1992/93	24	12	58	22	25
1993/94	23	11	59	22	24

Source: Government Statistical Service, 1996.[31]

KEY MESSAGES

A third of dependent children are living in poverty.

The proportion of lone parents on a low income is rising.

Households with children are at greatest risk of poverty.

Poverty in the 1990s includes a lack of 'necessities' as basic as food.

POVERTY AND DISABILITY IN YOUNG PEOPLE

Forty thousand children in the UK have been estimated to have severe learning difficulties.[40] Many young people with learning difficulty have multiple disabilities. This places great demands on families and carers, many of whom do not receive the practical, financial and social support that they need. Many parents who have cared for their child during childhood become distressed when they discover how difficult it has become to obtain residential accommodation for their children. This problem becomes serious as young people approach early adulthood and lose the support available from the education system.[40]

There are many problems associated with assessing the extent of disability both among the population as a whole and in relation to young people. An integral part of this problem is defining what is meant by the term 'disability' which has become something of a catchall term covering everything from difficulty with reading to severe, multiple physical disability. The use of 'disability' as a generic term is unsatisfactory, but what appears to be common to all those labelled as 'disabled', 'handicapped' or having 'special needs' is that they are excluded from the category of 'able-bodied' because they are in some way different and are, to a greater or lesser extent, marginalised from their peers and wider society.[41] The National Child Development Study (NCDS) questionnaire definition of chronic illness or disability, as limiting everyday activities, is the broad definition applied here.[42] However, there is a wide range of research which suggests that society, environmental factors and socioeconomic status interact together to make someone 'disabled' rather than this being the straightforward product of their 'condition'. The psychosocial effects of disability itself can be considerable, but these are frequently accentuated by social exclusion and stigma.[15]

The official estimate of the number of young people under 16 with disability is in excess of 300,000 but only 23,000 are actually registered as disabled. Of those who are registered, 5,600 are described as 'severely or appreciably handicapped', yet OPCS estimates the actual number in this category to be 29,000.[29] Research into 'benefit reach' (the extent to which the eligibility for benefit is matched by benefit receipt) suggests that the use of OPCS locomotion scales shows how widespread the inconsistencies in awards are.[43]

Social class affects uptake of specialist clinics dealing with chronic illness such as cystic fibrosis,[44] and it can be argued that the factor which has the greatest influence on early mortality in young people with cystic fibrosis is social class. There is a disproportionate failure in uptake of specialist services (medical and ancillary) among lower socioeconomic groups. This may be due to:

- a lack of resources to visit specialist centres/services;
- a lack of financial resources for special dietary needs and/or supplements;
- poor/overcrowded housing and environment;
- lower educational achievement.

Households where there is a disabled child have only 78 per cent of the resources of all families with children.[13] This makes any special needs a young person may have more difficult to provide.[45] For carers, even when their dependant dies, leaves home or enters an institution, the likelihood of their being able to re-enter the labour market and regain lost income and career prospects is very low.

The Children's Act (1989) clearly states that local authorities must provide for disabled children and young people with '... services designed to minimise the effect on disabled children of their disabilities and give them the opportunity to lead lives that are as normal as possible'.[46] As with other aspects of health, therefore, it appears that young people with disability would benefit from more specific rather than generic policies. This concurs with the recommendations of the *Griffiths Report* (1988) which states that community care plans should be tailored to meet individual needs. To organisations such as Sense, the most important aspect of community care is the opportunity to '... buy in more *appropriate services* ... to provide more specific packages of care'.[47]

Sense is an organisation whose client group consists of children and adults of all ages, with multiple, sensory disability. Some of Sense's young clients also have profound learning difficulties, other physical disabilities or a combination of some or all of these. But many of the day-to-day problems experienced by young people who use Sense can be applied to the more general experience of young people with other types of disability. For Sense, the most important aspects of care for young people (and their carers) are:

- planning for young people's transition to adulthood in order to maximise each young person's potential and, where appropriate, to negotiate an extended period of transition which goes beyond the 'official' definition of childhood. (This is with the support from the Further Education Funding Council);
- to act as an advocate for the young person and their carer/s;
- to fulfil the '... basic human right to care needs';
- to provide care regardless of ability to pay;
- to overcome the '... bureaucrats [who] become gatekeepers to opportunities'.

KEY MESSAGE

Poverty poses special problems for disabled young people and their families.

YOUNG PEOPLE IN INSTITUTIONAL CARE

Every year approximately 10,000 young people leave care to live 'independent' lives. Under normal circumstances they are eligible to leave care at the age of 16, but often they have little or no choice regarding when they leave. Many young people feel that society stigmatises them because they have been in care and feel that society is not well informed about the various routes into care – death of a parent, parental illness, breakdown of family relationships or as a place of safety due to abuse – and often assumes that young people who are, or were in care have behavioural problems for which they were receiving punishment.[48]

Here we aim to focus on the effect of leaving care on a young person's health. In 1995 Save the Children commissioned ten young people who had been in care, to research what had been the most problematic issues for them when they left care.[48] One of the areas referred to by them all was health. But good health and healthy living are prioritised among many other needs: one interviewee said, 'You don't think about your health when you are on the street.' Overall, the young people who were interviewed by their peers were concerned about their health yet had little information on how and where they could find help and advice on:

- registering with a doctor;
- how to use hospitals;
- the best way to shop for food and how to cook;
- alcohol and drug use; and
- sex and contraception.

Research refers to young people who become ill, unaware that they need to be registered with a medical practice or how to contact a doctor.[49] For some young people there is so little support, or information on how to access services, they have to resort to quite desperate measures which injure their mental, physical and psychological wellbeing.

> when I left care my support died on me. After I took an overdose I got more help.[48]

'Young people from care … are expected to be capable of independent living at a younger age than their contemporaries from a parental home' – yet they have far fewer support networks than their peers.[49] Preparation for independent living on leaving care has become an important issue over the last ten years. Section 24 (1) of the Children Act 1989 states that :'Where a child is being looked after by the local authority, it shall be the duty of the authority to advise, assist and befriend him with a view to promoting his welfare when he ceases to be looked after by them'.[50]

Young people in or leaving care do not, generally, achieve the same educational level as their peers.[51] This is often due to the numerous moves between homes, which often involves changing schools, that young people in care can experience. John Triseliotis and colleagues put this in context and say it is hardly surprising that so many young people from care have such an unsuccessful transition into adulthood:'... few people with good material and social supports attempt to manage on their own at 16–17 years'.[49]

Housing is frequently another major problem. Save the Children's 1994 report estimates that 40 per cent of homelessness among 16 and 17 year olds is the direct result of leaving care.[52] Yet those young people who have least invested in them are, it appears, expected to have the capacity to cope on their own at 16. Figure 1.2 clearly demonstrates that both men and women leaving care have to assume independent accommodation between three and four years earlier than their peers.

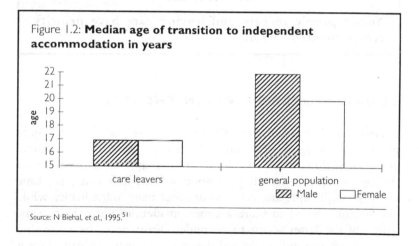

Figure 1.2: **Median age of transition to independent accommodation in years**

Source: N Biehal, et al., 1995.[51]

One in seven young women leaving care, and interviewed in a 1992 study, was pregnant or already had children.[50] This high number of pregnant young women may be influenced by their exposure/ vulnerability to sexual exploitation, their acceptance of affection from inappropriate adults and the adoption of motherhood as a source of identity.[49, 51, 52, 53]

One young man (interviewed for a Nuffield Foundation project investigating homelessness among young Black people) described his experience of leaving care:'I was 16 years of age, in care ... One day they [social services] packed up some of my things, put me in a car and dropped me off at a hostel'.[54] It can be further noted that:

- young people of mixed race are two and half times more likely than their white contemporaries to enter care; and
- young Black people who are cared for outside an institution often feel doubly stigmatised, because, if their carer is white, they are quite conspicuously being 'looked after'.[51]

It appears that the most important physical and psychological health-related issues for young people leaving care are:

- maintaining relationships with key workers;
- knowing how to register with a 'family' doctor;
- access to, and knowledge of, young people's clinics;
- developing and maintaining personal identity.

KEY MESSAGE

Young people in care and leaving care have priority requirements to be met.

YOUNG PEOPLE'S LIVES IN THE 1990s

Society has changed dramatically over the last few decades. Young people are trying to grow up and strive for security in a rapidly evolving world and some problems are common to all members of this age group, whether they are poor or not. Adolescence is a time when young people are trying to discover their individuality, while also having a need to share a common identity with their peers. Much of the latter seems to be under threat from the increasing emphasis on the individual and the quest for material gain. This is compounded by the fact that for the first time in many generations, the youth of today cannot assume that their standard of living will be higher than that of their parents.

A recent ICM Poll of 500 children between the ages of 11 and 15 suggests that young people's concerns are very much tied up with their hopes and aspirations for the future.[55] For example, 72 per cent referred to employment prospects as their greatest concern and over 60 per cent were concerned about the environment. Interviews carried out for this book confirm the same concerns about the future.

> **Young people's experience of poverty in 1990s Britain**
>
> *Jed's story* (aged 16)
> 'I've been living in a tent for six months. It's hard at first to fall asleep. It's cold but you get used to it.'
> (Guardian, 14 October 1995)
>
> *Sweet sixteen – bitter, bored and abandoned*
> 'I will do anything, I've got to get work.' A tear trickled down her face. 'I'm not clever enough, you need A levels. What can I do?'
> (Observer, 23 July 1995)
>
> *18 year-old mother with 2 year-old daughter*
> 'Make them understand … I've got £40 a week, how do I manage?'
>
> *14 year-old student at comprehensive school*
> 'We should be able to choose what we want to eat if we get free dinners – you have to have the set meal, you can't choose for yourself'. I'd like to taste more low fat meals … the different fruit and veg and that … but it's expensive … some of it's not for the likes of us.'
> Interviews for this research

YOUTH CULTURE, POVERTY AND EXCLUSION

By the 80s 'Youth Culture' had become an industry in itself and it was even argued by some that youth was no longer about rebellion or revolt but constituted merely a marketing device and advertisers' fiction.[56]

If you don't look good you can get tormented at school….if you wear old track suit bottoms without a name on them like Adidas, you get bullied.[55]

Since 1979 consumption appears to have come to play an increasingly active role in young people's lives – regardless of gender or ethnicity. Common identity, it may be argued, is under threat from the influence of the mass media. These have probably become the single most important source of culture for today's generation and their enormous power both unites and divides. Young people are constantly bombarded with ever-changing images and fashions which they may feel pressured into conforming with so as to fit in with their 'mates'.[57] Bullying, for example, a common problem reported by 63 per cent in the *Guardian* ICM poll, is often not just associated with physical appearance but also with clothing. The nature of one's footwear, particularly for boys, seems to hold particular significance. Teenagers thought it was right to spend around £70 on trainers, a figure obviously way beyond the scope of families on a low income struggling to buy necessities. Similarly, young males frequently demand the latest football team kit, which changes on an annual basis. The current cost of the whole kit is over £50. Many of the areas with the biggest following of football fans (a significant proportion of whom are in the 11–19 age category) are located in deprived regions such as Merseyside and the North East.

Young women are targeted for different consumer products, most of which are portrayed as enhancing body image. However, these products are as much a uniform of belonging as the football kits referred to above. The most powerful, and perhaps most alarming, aspect of image making through the media is the transient nature of images of beauty – a term which appears to be as problematic as health and poverty. But these images are dependent to a great extent on money, and the ability to buy the necessary commodities.

The images of ideal types are frequently thinner than up to 95 per cent of women who see them and this 'culture of thinness' appears to encourage young women to strive for an 'attractive' rather than a 'healthy' body size.[58] This is not to suggest that young women respond automaton-like to media images promoting commodities, but they have their icons in the same way that footballers are emulated by young men. There is, for example, a growing trend for bands led by women to have female fans who start their own fashion or 'look'. This was explained by one singer who said: 'People in certain bands have their own identities, as opposed to fashion models who just wear the clothes they're given' (Sarah Cracknell of Saint Etienne, quoted in the *Guardian*). However, it still costs money to emulate these singers, as it does to belong to any part of youth culture. Music has always played an important role in youth culture. Most of the gang cultures over the years have been primarily linked to the prevailing music scene.

YOUTH CULTURE AND GENDER DIFFERENCES IN LEISURE ACTIVITIES

Leisure activities seem to be undergoing a period of transition. During the 1980s, computer games such as Nintendo were all the rage but more than half the young people surveyed now spend an hour or less on them. Sports such as snooker have become very popular with boys, again reflecting the power of television. The average time spent watching television is 12 hours per week, the most of any activity asked about. Interestingly, some of the boys who undertake more active sports do not smoke because they think it will affect their performance. Sixty-four per cent read for an hour or less per week outside school. Social class appears to have little effect on reading patterns, but girls have a much more positive attitude to reading than do boys.[55]

YOUTH CULTURE AND MEDIA INFLUENCES ON SMOKING BEHAVIOUR

Much of the contemporary research on young people and smoking suggests that young people are well aware of the risks associated with smoking but those who are smokers are less likely than their non-smoking contemporaries to rate the risks as important.[2, 13, 56] Young people who smoke believe that the factors which have the greatest effect on their life expectancy are '... having a job and exercise'.[59] The influence of tobacco advertising through sport sponsorship and widespread media attention was evident among a survey of 11 to 16 year olds:

- 35 per cent of young people linked motor racing to cigarette advertising (Marlboro and Rothmans);
- 30 per cent made an association between darts and cigarettes (Embassy);
- 28 per cent associated snooker with cigarettes (Embassy and Benson & Hedges);
- 18 per cent associated cricket with cigarettes (Benson & Hedges).

Source: Survey carried out by MORI for Action on Smoking and Health (Ash) 1996.[60]

Over one-third of the teenage smokers agreed with the statement that '... smoking can't be all that dangerous or the Government would ban sports sponsorship by tobacco companies'.[60] A majority of the young smokers interviewed thought higher prices would have deterred them from smoking and that it would deter other young people.

Temporal trends suggest that taking up smoking is increasing faster for 15 year old girls (from 20 to 26 per cent) than boys (from 16 to 18 per cent).[61] This difference may reflect sporting activities among boys and the observation that girls saw smoking as a way to curb appetite and stay slim.[62]

Buying cigarettes does not appear to be difficult for young people. Over 50 per cent of 11–15 year olds interviewed by the HEA thought it was easy to buy cigarettes from newsagents.[62] Young men interviewed said it depended how tall they were or whether an older friend would buy them. It was also possible to buy them loose rather than in packets which overcame some of the problems of cost but was obviously less economical in the long run.

SEX AND DRUGS – AN INTEGRAL PART OF YOUTH CULTURE?

Sexual activity and use of drugs among 11 to 15 year olds

Two-thirds have had a boyfriend or girlfriend.

One-quarter of 15 year olds and 10% of 14 year olds have had sexual intercourse.

Sex before the age of consent is very common – it's twice as common among working-class as middle-class young people.

80% have had an alcoholic drink.

90% were given the drink by their parents or another relative.

Almost 50% of 15 year olds have drunk alcohol in a pub without their parents.

One in three has been drunk – figure rises to 45% among 13-15 year olds.

Three-quarters get cigarettes from friends – one-third regularly buy them in shops.

49% of girls smoke regularly compared to 39% of boys.

Nearly 25% have taken drugs.

24% have been offered glue or solvents.

One-third have been offered drugs – 10% have taken them (80% of whom took them more than once).

Source: ICM Poll, 1996.[55]

Teenage boys generally take far greater risks with their health and wellbeing than their female counterparts ... among certain groups of boys, and they can be from any background, larking around ... is a way of proving themselves to their friends, establishing a pecking order, and enhancing a reputation with members of the opposite sex.[63]

Adolescence is a period when many young people start experimenting in different ways. Although the number of young people who try drugs does not vary greatly according to class, it is generally the case that those from higher socioeconomic groups tend to experiment for a shorter period of time with a wider range of drugs, while young people with lower socioeconomic status appear to be more vulnerable to addiction. Young males, in particular, take many risks with their health. This may be for a number of reasons including the desire to be seen as being one of the gang or as being 'hard' to their friends. The same sort of pressures affect girls: for example, having lots of boyfriends at an early age may signal a girl's attractiveness and femininity.

> The availability of drugs is one of the main experiences that distinguishes this generation from previous ones.[55]

In recent years there appears to have been a significant increase in the availability of drugs in secondary schools. Almost every child who was interviewed confirmed they knew of drugs being taken. This was true in all areas of the country and, like alcohol consumption, it is not just a problem of inner-city deprivation, and appears to cross social classes. Although recent research suggests that young people of lower socioeconomic position are significantly more likely to be offered drugs, they are no more likely to take them than their better-off contemporaries. The quote referred to above suggests that the 1990s drug 'problem' is unique, inasmuch as drugs are, apparently, freely available. It may be that the drugs 'problem' has remained the same but it is now more acceptable to discuss it openly in schools, at home, in the media and with health professionals than it was in the 1960s, '70s and '80s. However, the availability of drugs in schools does appear to be far more commonplace in the 1990s than it was in previous decades.

> *Most people realise the dangers [of drugs] without being told.*
>
> Michael, aged 15

> *We probably know more than the teachers anyway [about drugs]. It's a joke to us really because they don't know what they're talking about.*
>
> Ben, aged 14

Young people seem aware of the dangers of drugs, although some of them mentioned that they would like more information about particular outcomes associated with named drugs. The drug of the early 1990s seems to have been Ecstasy or 'E' as it is commonly known. Ecstasy is associated with rave culture and the rise in popularity of acid house music in the mid- and late-1980s. It is now widespread among many social groups and is the introduction for many young people into the world of illicit drug use. It still has the image among many club goers as a 'friendly' drug but this may have been tempered by the well-publicised death of the teenager, Leah Betts, who died after taking 'E' in a Colchester nightclub. Everybody interviewed in the *Guardian* survey either mentioned her in connection with drugs or had at least heard of her.

YOUTH CULTURE IN A MULTI-CULTURAL SOCIETY

We refer above to 'youth culture' as if all young people share the same experience and that financial differences are more stressful than other distinguishing factors. But for many young people ethnicity compounds the effects of low income and creates a poverty of opportunity and aspiration. Despite Britain's race relations legislation, social and institutional racism persist.

Once young people have run the gamut of abuse at school and enter the job market they then have to overcome obstacles as simple as having a name which can be distinguished as non-British, culturally biased psychometric tests or other forms of covert racism. Young people from ethnic minorities are twice as likely as their white counterparts to be unemployed. Even among prestigious jobs such as law there appear to be marked discrepancies in the success of white and Black students – white law students have a 47 per cent chance of taking articles compared with only 7 per cent of Black students.[64-67]

Young people of mixed race can suffer double jeopardy and be excluded by both communities. Olumide describes this experience as '... a feature of the "mixed race condition" that people in mixed race families are simply not perceived as belonging together'.[68] But young people want to belong, conform and compete with their peers on an equal basis regardless of race, colour or creed.

YOUTH CULTURE AND THE EXPERIENCE OF YOUNG PEOPLE WITH A DISABILITY

Disability takes many forms and may be physical or mental. As far as the latter is concerned '... mental health is much more than simply the absence of mental illness ... the mental health of young people is essentially about their emotional well-being'.[69] Both poverty and racism can profoundly affect psychological wellbeing.

It is not 'disability' in itself which is disabling but the environment in which young people find themselves, the attitudes of others, exclusion from activities and the labelling process of actually being called 'disabled' because one looks or behaves in a different way.

The experience of being disabled differs according to income, and financial resources can make a profound difference to mobility, care and buying in of services.[70,71] As far as care services are concerned, a disproportionate amount of these are used by the higher socio-economic classes while for minority ethnic groups it is often assumed that external services are not required because an extended family exists that is willing and able to carry out all aspects of care.[72]

Once again we can see that young people may share the same aspirations but that the means to achieve is not equitably divided.

KEY MESSAGES

The experience of young people in contemporary British society differs according to class, ethnicity and/or gender.

Advertising which is targeted at young people contributes to both financial and health inequalities.

Young people are concerned about their future as independent young adults.

THE TRANSITION FROM CHILDHOOD TO ADULTHOOD – AN ARTIFICIAL DIVIDE

When we hear the word 'capital' we may think of wealth and the capital and estates inherited from generation to generation. But it is not only financial capital that we inherit. The concept of 'social capital' embraces the notion of norms, values, knowledge, expectations, hopes, aspirations and life chances which are also passed on through generations by parental education and encouragement.

Over the last 30 years, figures suggest that there has been a significant rise in living standards for the country as a whole. Nevertheless, the rise in 'average' earnings or disposable income is distorted by the disproportionate growth in prosperity experienced by the richest in society. The same may be argued about inherited social capital, particularly over the last 17 years.[73,74] As we approach the 21st century it is becoming more and more apparent that young people do not experience the same inter-generational inheritance of capital, social or otherwise. Consequently this has a profound effect on many young people's transition into the adult world and towards becoming independent.

TRANSITION AND EDUCATION

The most empowering investment young people can make in themselves is education, one of the key passports out of poverty.[21] But the notion of meritocracy and a so-called level playing field in educational access is somewhat fallacious. Inherited wealth and parental socioeconomic status are strongly correlated with educational opportunities.[21, 68] Education is particularly important because it is an integral part of the social capital each of us carries (as an asset or a burden) throughout our lives and is used as a passport into tertiary education, secure permanent employment and other integral aspects of our lives which have a profound affect on our health status and vulnerability to health and illness.[75] It is between the ages of 11 and 19 that most of us invest in our education, gaining secondary qualifications and skills for further education or employment as young adults. However, young people's ability to invest in their lives during this period is, to a great extent, constrained by earlier life, environmental and educational experiences. Household poverty may further constrain educational attainment if, for example, poverty means a lack of basic items for homework.[21] This may be particularly relevant for young people in temporary, usually cramped housing. Financial circumstances are, of course, not the only aspect of a young person's life that affects investment in their social capital throughout their younger years. But what is apparent is that poverty affects a range of other resources which are made available to young people during their transition to adulthood, and influence their educational attainment.

> We do help with the cost of uniforms and extras ... but we have had pupils who have refused free school meals ... one boy said he would rather go without.
>
> Bursar at an Independent Grammar School

> Hungry children don't learn.
>
> National Food Alliance, 1996

Young people from poor circumstances whose abilities are recognised may gain assisted places at independent schools. But they will have far more social and economic hurdles to clear than their more affluent contemporaries. They may not be able to afford to socialise with their peers and feel excluded and it is probable that they are dependent on schools to assist with the cost of uniforms and 'extras'.[3, 21, 73] If their families are on income support (IS) they will be entitled to free school meals but research suggests that not being poor enough to qualify for IS can also be an impoverishing experience. Many young people experience the double jeopardy of being poor, but not quite poor enough for free school meals. However, qualifying for means-tested benefits is also seen as a stigmatising process.[21, 66] A 'them and us' ethos exists with means-tested benefits, and interviews with young people who are entitled to free school meals and their mothers reveal that this is exactly what happens in practice.

> *Mothers at a Barnardo's Family Centre:*
> My three have free dinners – they want packed lunches like their friends ... I can't afford them ... sometimes I do them as a treat.
>
> If I could afford them [school dinners] then my girl would like them but because we are not on family credit we don't get free dinners.

It is estimated that 20 per cent of households entitled to free school meals do not claim them. But this does not tell us how many young people are in the households that are entitled to school dinners. The percentage of young people who go without therefore is probably much higher than the household figure suggests. Evidence from young people, parents and schools suggests that poverty excludes and denies choice and autonomy in something as basic as food. In addition, the mother quoted above, who is not poor enough to be on family credit, raises the important issue of what happens to those households living on the poverty line.[3] The prime purpose of benefits is to give protection against poverty and not poverty alleviation.[76] It may be argued that providing a meal for a young person at lunchtime would be quite a protective measure.

> ... the right of every child to a standard of living adequate for the child's physical, mental, spiritual, moral and social development.
>
> Article 27[1]

Social exclusion at school due to poverty which does not allow for 'extras' or simply wearing the same clothes as one's contemporaries has a profound affect on educational achievement.[21] The consensual view of poverty defines these everyday expenses as part of the necessities of life.[37] A study on the inheritance of poverty and affluence showed successful, high-earning sons are '... much more likely to have had high-earning fathers than low-earning fathers'.[77] Educational under-achievement and poor employment prospects are inextricably linked to poor socioeconomic circumstances, insecure, low paid employment and unemployment, all of which appear to have a profound effect on health status in adult life.[14, 15, 78, 79]

If young people from low income households do manage to overcome all these obstacles and proceed into higher education, they then have to be able to afford to get into debt. If you are poor already, credit costs you more.[80] The average student owes approximately £1,982; in excess of 50 per cent of undergraduates receive an average of £51 per week from their parents; one in five receives a lump sum from parents of £800+.[81] In 1992/3, 47 per cent of households living in poverty were couples with children and recent findings by the Joseph Rowntree Foundation suggest that families on benefit need an additional £15 per week to be able to buy such basics as food and fuel.[82] It is unlikely that parents in low income households could achieve these additional payments for their children. Despite this, Prince Charles contends that:

> Poor economic circumstances should not be an excuse for failure. As I myself see, visiting schools in some of the poorest and most deprived parts of cities, poverty is not a bar to excellence and achievement.[83]

TRANSITION AND EMPLOYMENT

> Most unemployed 16 and 17 year olds cannot get Income Support. Instead the Government guarantee a place on Youth Training (YT). This may be the only source of income for young people, and yet many still regard the schemes with suspicion, and there is no guarantee of a job at the end.[84]

When young people are asked what they want most when they leave school the most common answer is 'a proper job' but many become disillusioned at being paid £1 an hour on training schemes that have no future for them.[85]

Over the last 15 years an estimated one to two hundred thousand 18–20 year olds have left continuing education, employment or training. These young people are described as 'disappointed, disadvantaged – disappeared'.[86] When we interviewed a group of young men and asked what worried them most about the future they said, 'getting a job', which they thought was going to become more difficult because the employment situation is 'going to get worse'.

Financial support is vital while seeking employment – it helps with clothes for interviews, self-esteem and finding somewhere to live for example. Young people also need to have the confidence to claim the benefits they are entitled to and other 'rights', such as freedom from exploitation.[84] Even though the majority of young people under 19 are now excluded from non-means-tested benefits, it should not be assumed that young people are able to rely on parents or guardians having the financial resources (or willingness) to provide for them financially. There is an association between unemployment and homelessness and homeless young people have few options in earning money. These young people are also extremely vulnerable to sexual exploitation and prostitution.[49, 87, 88]

For many young people, contributing to domestic economy in 'services' such as baby sitting or as unpaid carers is part of their everyday lives. They may also contribute to household expenses through legal earnings from a paper round perhaps or through illegal and often dangerous employment. The notion of all young people as economically dependent is quite misleading and the assumption often conceals the problem of an artificially rapid transition into employment which prevents many young people from investing in themselves. Those who end up in low paid, insecure employment pay for their poverty with years of their lives.[89]

It appears then that poverty affects education and employment opportunities and it can also hasten an artificially rapid transition into economic responsibility for others in the domestic sphere.

TRANSITION AND HOUSING

There appears to be an overwhelming assumption that 'leaving home' will be the same experience for all young people. However, a growing number of young people (mostly male) are delaying their transition into independent living and staying at home even if attending university.[90] But not all young people have this choice. Those leaving care have little or no choice of when and how this transition will take place.[86] The reality for many young people is that independent living, particularly when there is a lack of financial and emotional support, can be an extremely daunting, dangerous and isolating experience which can have a profound effect on mental, physical and psychological wellbeing. Access to secure, safe housing can also dictate whether a young person is able to find employment as an address is required for all job applications. Shelter is a basic need and Article 27 of the UN Convention of the Rights of the Child states that we are collectively responsible for providing

> ... material assistance and support programmes particularly with regard to nutrition, clothing and housing.

We, as a society, appear to fail on the latter, particularly in the provision of housing for young people who do not have affluent parents or independent means and young people who are leaving care.[91-93]

It is estimated that, in 1990, 43,000 young people ran away from home over 100,000 times.

180,000 British children experience homelessness each year.

A disproportionate number of young people who have been in institutional care become homeless.

In 1995 the Government announced plans to check with parents before paying benefits to young people.

Many young people who run away from home are running away from abuse.

Only a minority of young people receive financial support in setting up their own home.

Over the last 15 years the housing of children in lone parent households has improved the least.

KEY MESSAGE

Education, employment and housing are essential components of a young person's transition to a healthy adult life.

SUMMARY

In Chapter 1 we have outlined the importance of examining the poverty experience of young people. This is a vital part of the life course which links childhood and adulthood. Young people's experience of poverty has a profound effect on mental, physical and psychological wellbeing and subsequent life chances.

The main messages in this chapter are:

- stereotypes can segregate, separate and isolate young people;
- young people's interpretation and experience of poverty is crucial, as is the impact on their sense of wellbeing, since this is the essence of health;
- the population of young people is set to increase;
- minority ethnic groups have a younger age distribution;
- one-third of dependent children are living in poverty;
- the proportion of lone parents on a low income is rising and households with children are at greatest risk of poverty;
- poverty in the 1990s includes a lack of 'necessities' as basic as food;
- poverty poses special problems for disabled young people and their families;
- young people in care and leaving care have priority requirements to be met;
- the experience of young people in contemporary British society differs according to class, ethnicity and/or gender, and is affected by advertising targeted at them that contributes to both financial and health inequalities;
- young people are concerned about their future as independent young adults; and
- education, employment and housing are essential components of a young person's transition to a healthy adult life.

NOTES

1. P Newell, *The UN Convention and Children's Rights in the UK*, National Children's Bureau,1991.
2. A Oakley, *et al.*, 'Health and cancer prevention: knowledge and beliefs of children and young people', *British Medical Journal*, 1995, 310: 1029–33.
3. C Oppenheim and L Harker, *Poverty: The Facts*, CPAG, 1996.
4. M Benzeval, K Judge and M Whitehead, *Tackling Inequalities in Health*, Kings Fund, 1995.
5. C Power, 'Social and economic background and class inequalities in health among young adults', *Social Science and Medicine*, 1991, 32: 411–17.
6. G Davey Smith, D Blane and M Bartley, 'Explanations for socio-economic differentials in mortality', *European Journal of Public Health*, 1994, 4: 131–44.

7. P Aggleton, *Management Summary of Promoting Young People's Health. The Health Concerns and Needs of Young People*, Health Education Authority, 1996.

8. S Macintyre and P West, 'Lack of class variation in health in adolescence: an artefact of an occupational measure of social class?', *Social Science and Medicine*, 1991, 32(4): 395–402.

9. P West, *et al.*, 'Social class and health in youth: findings from the west of Scotland Twenty-07 Study', *Social Science and Medicine*, 1990, 30: 665–73.

10. M Rutter and D J Smith, *Psychosocial Disorders in Young People*, John Wiley and Sons, 1995.

11. D P Strachan, 'Ventilatory function as a predictor of fatal stroke', *British Medical Journal*, 1991, 302: 84–7.

12. NCH Maternity Alliance, *Poor Expectations*, NCH Action for Children and The Maternity Alliance, 1995.

13. C Woodroffe, *Children, Teenagers and Health*, Macmillan, 1993.

14. G Davey Smith and J Morris, 'Increasing inequalities in the health of the nation', *British Medical Journal*, 1994, 309: 1453–4.

15. N Spencer, *Poverty and Child Health*, Routledge, 1996.

16. A Steptoe and N Butler, 'Sports participation and emotional wellbeing in adolescents', *Lancet*, 1996, 347: 1789–92.

17. General Household Survey, *Living in Britain: Results from the 1994 General Household Survey*, HMSO, 1994.

18. J Haskey, 'The ethnic minority populations of Great Britain: their estimated sizes and age profiles', *Population Trends*, 1996, 84.

19. B Armitage, 'Population review – Structure and distribution of the population', *Population Trends*, 1995, 81.

20. I Gilmour, *Dancing with Dogma. Britain under Thatcherism*, Pocket Books, 1993.

21. T Smith and M Noble, *Education Divides*, CPAG, 1995.

22. J Mack and S Lansley, *Poor Britain*, Allen and Unwin, 1985.

23. P Townsend, *Poverty in the UK: A Survey of Household Resources and Standards of Living*, Penguin, 1979.

24. R G Wilkinson, 'Divided we fall: the poor pay the price of increased social inequality', *British Medical Journal*, 1994, 308: 1113–14.

25. R G Wilkinson, *Unhealthy Societies: The Afflictions of Inequality*, Routledge, 1996.

26. Joseph Rowntree Foundation, *Inquiry into Income and Wealth. Volume 1*, in the Barclay Report, 1995.

27. Barnardo's, *Too Much Too Young: The failure of Social Policy in Meeting the Needs of Care Leavers*, Barnardo's, 1996.

28. Barnardo's, *Transition to adulthood*, Barnardo's, 1996.

29. NCH, *Children in Britain*, The NCH Factfile, 1992.

30. C Oppenheim, *Poverty: The Facts*, CPAG, 1993.

31. Government Statistical Service: *Households Below Average Income. A Statistical Analysis 1979–1992/92*, Department of Social Security, 1996.

32. J Bradshaw, *Child Poverty and Deprivation in the UK*, National Children's Bureau, 1990.

33. V Kumar, *Poverty and Inequality in the UK – the Effects on Children*, National Children's Bureau, 1993.

34. A E Green, *The Geography of Poverty and Wealth*, Institute of Employment Research, 1994.

35. A E Green, 'Aspects of the changing geography of poverty and wealth', in J Hilla, *New Inequalities: The Changing Distribution of Income and Wealth in the United Kingdom*, Cambridge University Press, 1996.

36. D Dorling, *A New Social Atlas of Britain*, John Wiley and Son, 1995.

37. D Gordon and C Pantazis (eds), *Breadline Britain in the 1990s: A Report to the Joseph Rowntree Foundation*, London Weekend Television, 1995.

38. A Atkinson, *Measuring poverty and differences in family composition*, London School of Economics, 1990.

39. D Gittins, *The Family in Question*, Macmillan, 1990.

40. C Cox and M Pearson, *Made to Care: The Case for Residential and Village Communities for People with a Mental Handicap*, The Rannoch Trust, 1995.

41. P Alcock, *Understanding Poverty*, Macmillan, 1993.

42. M Barker and C Power, 'Disability in young adults: the role of injuries', *Journal of Epidemiology and Community Health* 1993, 47: 349-54.

43. M Daly and M Noble, 'The reach of disability benefits: an examination of the disability living allowance', *Journal of Social Welfare and Family Law*, 1996, 18: 37-51.

44. J R Britton, 'Effects of social class, sex, and region of residence on age at death from cystic fibrosis', *British Medical Journal*, 1989, 298: 483-7.

45. J Preece, 'Class and disability: influences on learning expectations', *Disability and Society*, 1996, 11: 191-204.

46. Children's Legal Centre, *The Children Act 1989*, The Children's Legal Centre, 1996.

47. D Harker, Effect of community care policies and the importance of transition planning for each young person. Telephone conversation, 28 August 1996.

48. Save the Children, *You're on Your Own: Young People's Research on Leaving Care*, Save the Children, 1995.

49. J Triseliotis, M Borland, M Hill and L Lambert, *Teenagers and the Social Work Services*, HMSO, 1995.

50. S Hutson and M Liddiard, *Youth Homelessness. The Construction of a Social Issue*, Macmillan, 1994.

51. N Biehal, J Clayden, M Stein and J Wade, *Moving On: Young People and Leaving Care Schemes*, HMSO, 1995.

52. Save the Children, *Lives of the Young and Homeless*, Save the Children, 1994.
53. M Stein, G Rees and N Frost, *Running the Risk. Young People on the Streets of Britain Today*, The Children's Society, 1994.
54. Nuffield Foundation, *Homelessness amongst Young Black Minority Ethnic People in England*, Research Findings, 1996.
55. The *Guardian*, 15 May 1996.
56. S Redhead, 'Rave off: politics and deviance in contemporary youth culture', *Popular Cultural Studies*, 1993, 1.
57. E Goffman, *Gender Advertisements*, Macmillan, 1979.
58. S Orbach, *Fat is a Feminist Issue: How to Lose Weight Permanently – Without Dieting*, Arrow Books, 1988.
59. J Brannen, *Young People, Health and Family Life*, Open University Press, 1994.
60. ASH, *Teenage Smokers*, Action on Smoking and Health, 1996.
61. M Stead, G Hastings and C Tudor-Smith, 'Preventing adolescent smoking: a review of options', *Health Education Journal*, 1996, 55: 31–54.
62. Health Education Authority, *Tackling Teenage Smoking*, HEA, 1995, part 1.6.
63. The *Independent*, 27 May 1996.
64. The *Guardian*, 20 April 1994.
65. The *Guardian*, 29 January 1996.
66. The *Guardian*, 23 July 1996.
67. E Murphy, *After the Asylums: Community Care for People with Mental Illness*, Faber and Faber Limited, 1991.
68. J Olumide, *The Social Construction of the 'Mixed Race Condition'*, BSA, 1996.
69. P Wilson, 'Working space: a mentally healthy young nation', *Youth and Policy*, 1995, 51: 60–3.
70. C Woodroffe and M Glickman, 'Trends in child health', *Children and Society*, 1993, 7(1): 49–63.
71. G Dalley, *Ideologies of Caring*, Macmillan, 1990.
72. Y Gunaratnam, *Call for Care*, Kings Fund, 1991.
73. A Quick and R Wilkinson, *Income and Health*, Socialist Health Association, 1991.
74. A Goodman and S Webb, *For Richer, For Poorer: The Changing Distribution of Income in the United Kingdom, 1961-91*, The Institute for Fiscal Studies, 1994.
75. M Young and A H Halsey, *Family and Community Socialism*, Institute for Public Policy Research, 1995.
76. F Bennett, *Social Insurance. Reform or Abolition?*, Institute for Public Policy Research, 1993.
77. P Johnson and H Reed, *Two Nations? The Inheritance of Poverty and*

Affluence, The Institute for Fiscal Studies, 1996.

78. W Hutton, *The State We're In*, Jonathan Cape, 1995.
79. M Bartley, 'Unemployment and ill health: understanding the relationship', *Journal of Epidemiology and Community Health*, 1994, 48: 333-7.
80. J Ford, *Consuming Credit: Debt and Poverty in the UK*, CPAG, 1991.
81. The *Guardian*, 6 July 1996.
82. E Kempson, *Life on a Low Income*, Joseph Rowntree Foundation, 1996.
83. The *Guardian*, 12 July 1996.
84. Children's Legal Centre, *At What Age Can I?* The Children's Legal Centre, 1996.
85. The *Observer*, 23 July 1995.
86. Young People Now, *Disappointed, Disadvantaged – Disappeared*, Young People Now, 1996.
87. P Aggleton .and I Warwick, *Young People, Homelessness and HIV/ AIDS*, Health Education Authority, 1992.
88. Children's Legal Centre, *The UN Convention on the Rights of the Child*, The Children's Legal Centre, 1996.
89. D Dorling, '£100 pay rise for low paid can hold key to longer life', The *Guardian*, 5 January 1996.
90. Children's Legal Centre, *Running Away: Leaving Parents without Consent*, The Children's Legal Centre, 1996.
91. *Young People's Transition to Adulthood*, Joseph Rowntree Foundation, 1996.
92. S Lowry, *Housing and Health*, BMJ Publications, 1991.
93. D Dorling, *Children and Housing in Britain: National Results from the Census*, Shelter, 1993.

The number of young people living in poverty has grown faster in the UK than in most European countries
Credit: Paula Solloway/Format

2 Ill health associated with poverty in young people

INTRODUCTION

In this chapter we consider the important causes of ill health, and sometimes death, in young people that have been shown to be particularly associated with poverty. Also included are examples of common diseases where there may be an association with poverty. The main health problems in young people that are associated with poverty are accidents, respiratory problems, depression, schizophrenia, suicide, eating disorders, sexually transmitted diseases, teenage pregnancy, and tobacco, alcohol and drug abuse. These health problems will have a long-term legacy which makes their prevention all the more important a challenge. Two diseases in young people where direct associations with poverty are not so clear, but where a direct effect on disease management can be seen, are asthma and diabetes. Mismanagement of these conditions will also risk a continuing legacy into adult life.

MORTALITY

In 1995 there were 1,840 deaths among people aged 10–19 in England and Wales, and yet between 1988 and 1995 there had been a general downward trend in mortality in young people and particularly in males. The exception is mortality from mental disorders, although only relatively small numbers are involved. In absolute terms, by far the biggest single cause of death among young people is from 'injury and poisoning', accounting for over half the deaths in 1992 (see Table 2.1).

TABLE 2.1: **Death rates per 100,000 population in young people aged 10–19, by ICD cause code, England and Wales, 1992**

	Males	Females
Injury and poisoning	25.12	9.19
Neoplasms	5.46	3.44
Nervous system	3.48	1.96
Mental disorders	1.75	0.49
Circulatory	1.69	1.37
Congenital	1.32	1.86
Endocrine and nutritional	1.09	0.84
Infectious and parasitic	0.96	0.98
Respiratory system	0.96	0.74
Other	0.26	0.28
Digestive system	0.23	0.32
Diseases of blood	0.20	0.18
Genito-urinary	0.13	0.07
Musculo-skeletal system	0.07	0.42
Total	42.73	22.12

Source: On the State of the Public Health, 1993.

Income and social class are strongly associated with health, children in [the lowest] unskilled manual households being twice as likely to die before the age of 15 years as children in the [highest] professional social class.[1]

A very important omission from most analyses is a group classified as 'unoccupied'.[2] Parents who are classified as 'unoccupied' largely consist of economically inactive single mothers. Children in the 'unoccupied' group have the worst mortality record of all social groups.[2] Those aged 10–15 have four times the relative risk of dying compared to social classes I and II.

The overreliance on occupational class as a mode of stratifying social groups has led to many studies mistakenly concluding that inequalities in mortality are less dramatic among young people than at other stages of the lifecycle.[2] However, when the mortality of all children is accounted for, '…inequalities are relatively consistent throughout childhood. In particular, they are much more substantial at ages 10–15 than is commonly supposed'.[2]

ACCIDENTS

Table 2.2 shows the predominance of transport accident deaths in the 10-14 age group and Figures 2.1 and 2.2 show the same for 15–19 year olds, with 376 transport accident deaths in young men and 110 in young women. There were 24 deaths from accidental poisoning in young men and 14 in young women, a large proportion of these almost certainly classifiable as suicides.

TABLE 2.2: **Deaths from accidental injuries and poisoning in young people aged 10–14, England and Wales, 1992**

	Male	Female
Transport accidents	85	50
Accidental poisoning	1	3
Accidental falls	13	0
Fire and flames	1	4
Accidental drowning	3	0
Inhalation	0	2
Others	5	1
Total	108	60

Note: ICD Codes E800-E849 are used in this table. Injuries caused by violence and self-harm are excluded. This definition is used in *The Health of the Nation: Key Area Handbook on Accidents* (DoH, 1993).[3]

Source: J Sibert, 1996.[3]

Social class differences in accident death rates

Children from the lowest social group have the highest risk of deaths for all types of accidents.[4]

Children aged 1-14 in households whose male 'head' is an unskilled manual worker are almost four times as likely to die from injuries…as children from professional households.[5]

Children in social class V are more than four times as likely to die as pedestrians than children in social class I.[6]

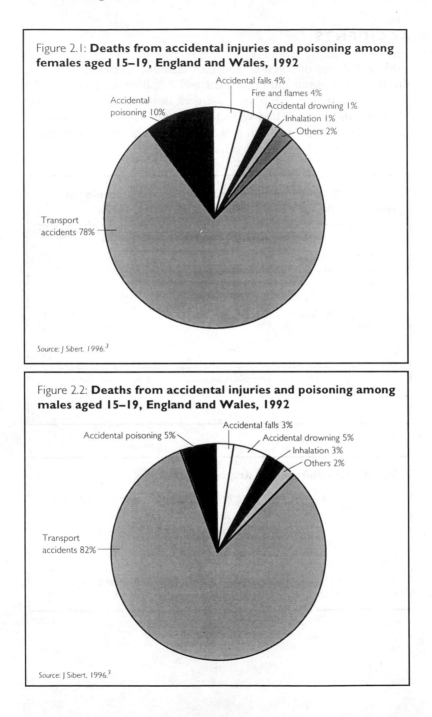

Figure 2.1: **Deaths from accidental injuries and poisoning among females aged 15–19, England and Wales, 1992**

Accidental falls 4%
Fire and flames 4%
Accidental drowning 1%
Inhalation 1%
Others 2%
Accidental poisoning 10%
Transport accidents 78%

Source: J Sibert, 1996.[3]

Figure 2.2: **Deaths from accidental injuries and poisoning among males aged 15–19, England and Wales, 1992**

Accidental falls 3%
Accidental drowning 5%
Inhalation 3%
Others 2%
Accidental poisoning 5%
Transport accidents 82%

Source: J Sibert, 1996.[3]

Deaths from unintentional injury have a steeper social class gradient than any other cause of death in childhood, particularly when the 'unoccupied' population is included. Death rates from injury and poisoning have declined for children aged 0–15 in all social classes between 1981 and 1991, but the decline for children in social classes IV and V (21 per cent and 2 per cent, respectively) is smaller than that for children in social classes I and II (32 per cent and 37 per cent, respectively).[7] The result is an increase in socioeconomic mortality differentials, with injury rates for children in social class V being five times that of children in social class I. If these trends continue, the Health of the Nation target is likely to be met by children in the non-manual social classes, but not by those in the manual social classes.[7] These figures are particularly depressing given that accidents are not truly random events but tend to occur in fairly predictable patterns. This implies that many of them are preventable.

TRAFFIC IN INNER-CITY AREAS

> We canna gan to the park. Cause if we gan that way it's too far and the traffic might knock you over. (Quote from child living in a deprived area of Newcastle)

> These roads are lethal. They [the joyriders] don't just come up there slow. They scream up there. (Parent in Newcastle)

> If you say to them right, you can't go from one side of the street to the other, it's like keeping them prisoners, they don't grow up to be independent. (Parent from Newcastle)

Not surprisingly, child pedestrian casualty rates are highest in deprived inner-city areas, and 95 per cent of child pedestrian and cyclist casualties occur in built-up areas. As well as having inferior facilities for playing, young people from poorer backgrounds generally have to contend with busier roads. The normal dangers of heavy traffic and parked cars are compounded by the problems of joyriding, which is not only a danger to those teenagers who participate in it, but also to other residents in the neighbourhood.

Towner, *et al.* (1994) tried to measure exposure to injury risk among affluent and deprived young people aged 11–14 who went to school in Newcastle.[8] Although some differences in risk are for evident reasons (poorer children were less likely to travel to school by car, be accompanied by an adult, or wear a seat belt), these aren't adequate for explaining the large social differences in accident rates. Despite the increase in traffic volume over the past two decades, child pedestrian death rates have fallen.[9] The decline seems to be primarily the result of a substantial reduction in children's traffic exposure, as a result of children being kept away from increasingly dangerous streets. The decline has been much less for the 5–14 age group, partly as a result of parents having more difficulty in limiting their exposure to traffic. Parents face a dilemma between trying to protect their children from the perils of heavy traffic and a generally dangerous environment, and the need to allow their children the independence they crave. Restricting children's traffic exposure denies children their right to mobility, especially those from less affluent backgrounds. A mobility restricting – as opposed to traffic calming – approach may also increase socioeconomic differentials in childhood mortality.[9]

PARENTAL SUPERVISION

Teenagers from the same area of Newcastle argue that it is unrealistic to expect children and young people to stay at home all the time and do things with their parents. What is needed are activities and facilities which are away from the streets. Furthermore, parents from poorer backgrounds are likely to have neither the resources nor the time to keep their children out of trouble, particularly if they are single parents. Indeed, children of lone mothers have injury rates that are twice those of children in two-parent families.[10] This discrepancy can be explained by the poverty, poor housing conditions, and social isolation of lone mothers in Britain.[10]

In overcrowded neighbourhoods which are lacking in safe places where children can play outside it is probably unrealistic to expect parents to provide constant supervision.[11] In a study of two areas in Yorkshire, one a deprived area with a high childhood accident rate and the other an affluent area with a low accident rate, significant differences emerged between the parents in each area in their expressed difficulty in keeping their children safe.[12]

MORBIDITY FROM ACCIDENTS

There are no overall national data for morbidity from accidents but there are various individual sources. For example, road traffic accident statistics are compiled from police report forms (STATS 19) but there are problems of underreporting of casualties, particularly involving cyclists.

Accidents are one of the most common causes of hospital admission in children aged 5–16.[4] Official hospital inpatient statistics for England for 1990–1991 show that 14.9 per 1,000 population for males and 10.7 per 1,000 population for females aged 5-14 were admitted for cases relating to injury and poisoning.[13] Overall, unintentional injury in childhood is the major cause of ill health in children (DoH, 1992). Evidence from Newcastle suggests that injury rates are highest in the 11-14 age group.[14] Less serious injuries are an important source of presentations to A&E departments. Figures for such presentations to the Cardiff Royal Infirmary for 14–18 year olds in 1993 are shown in Table 2.3. The number of presentations during the year was 5,410.

TABLE 2.3: **Accident and emergency presentations of 14–18 year olds, Cardiff Royal Infirmary, 1993**

Type of injury	%	Place of injury	%
Accident	53.6	Home	29.9
Sport	17.6	Public place	26.5
Assault	6.8	Sport	18.1
Medical	6.3	Education	13.0
Self-injury	2.2	Work	4.0
Other	13.5	Road traffic accidents	3.4
		Other	5.1

Source: *Injuries to Adolescents*, RCP, 1996.[15]

The social differences in accident rates are not simply a result of the use of class differences in the use of A&E facilities.[14] It is a real phenomenon. Hospital admission data are a good indicator of morbidity but the decision of the patient to attend the hospital and the decision of the doctor to admit the patient are both affected by, among other things, social class. Those in the lower social classes are less likely to be admitted, which leads to an underestimate of social class differentials.[14] Among children aged 0–16 in three northeast health districts, a linear relationship existed between age and the frequency of severe injuries, with older children having more cases per year of severe injury. Areas with higher levels of social deprivation had the highest rates for injuries. Compared to the most affluent wards, the most deprived wards had 2.4 times more injuries of any kind, 3.6 times more severe injuries, and 7.5 times more deaths. Not only is the rate of accidental injury higher in poorer areas but also poorer areas are more likely to have the more severe injuries.[14]

Evidence from the 1958 birth cohort estimated that the prevalence of permanent disability at the age of 23 following an injury was 28 per 1,000.[16] Another study estimated that about 3 per cent of children under 15 years admitted to hospital after an accident are left with a permanent disability.[5]

Alcohol is a contributory factor in at least 30 per cent of accidents for all age groups. It has also been estimated that alcohol contributes to at least 60 per cent of fatal accidents in young men occurring between 10pm and 4am.[11] The consumption of alcohol in combination with high risk activities, such as driving too fast, may be part of a constellation of risk taking behaviour. This will be discussed further below.

KEY MESSAGE

Young people in poverty suffer more accidents causing deaths and injury.

PREVALENCE OF ILL HEALTH

Mortality data alone are relatively poor indicators of health status among younger people as death is comparatively rare in this age group. There is a dearth of information about social class and general health or morbidity among young people. Morbidity is difficult to assess in this age group because of its self-reported nature and the fact that a good deal of childhood morbidity is reported by parents. In addition to this, young people are usually regarded as being healthy individuals who make few demands on the health service. For young people from lower social classes, there is also a possibility that morbidity is underreported. Research among adults demonstrates that individuals with less education tend to report less chronic illness than those with more education as compared to doctor diagnoses.[17] This would lead to the attenuation of socioeconomic gradients in morbidity if self-report data were used.

The self-reported prevalence of both longstanding and limiting longstanding illness, reported in the General Household Survey, has increased among 5–15 year olds since 1979. For this age group, figures vary little by social class. Among adults, however, there is quite substantial variation by social class.[18]

The 'West of Scotland Twenty-07 Cohort Study' is an extensive study of the social patterning of health in the Central Clydeside Conurbation (CCC), an area characterised by pockets of severe deprivation.[19] In comparison with findings from various other British health surveys, little or no difference exists between CCC and Britain as a whole in rates of longstanding and limiting longstanding illness among young people. However, marked differences emerge at mid- and later middle life with those in CCC coming off worse.[19] The other major finding to emerge was the relative disadvantage in terms of self-rated health (health in the past 12 months) and psychological wellbeing among younger people in CCC compared to their peers in other areas. The relatively high rates of youth unemployment was suggested as the major contributory factor to these poorer levels of psychosocial health.

GP CONSULTATIONS

In 1994 one-tenth of those aged 5–15 had consulted with a GP in the 14 days before interview, and the average number of consultations per person per year in this age group was three. These figures have changed very little since 1979, and vary little by social class. Further evidence is available from surveys of Morbidity Statistics from General Practice.[20] For those aged 5–15 and 16–24, respiratory tract diseases are the major cause of consultation. Both age groups showed an increase in overall patient consulting rates between 1981– 1982 and 1991–1992 (figures should be treated with some caution as age bands were changed between the two reference points, as were survey conditions and methods). Table 2.4 shows age standardised patient consulting ratios (SPCRs) by social class of parent (figures should again be treated with some caution as the confidence limits around some of the figures are very large and the major part of the age band is for children , not young people).Although the SPCR for all diseases taken together is very similar across the social classes, there are some significant differences within the individual categories of illness and disease. SPCRs tend to be higher among the lower social classes for categories other than neoplasms and diseases of the nervous system.

TABLE 2.4: **Age standardised patient consulting ratios (SPCR) for children aged 0–15: comparison by sex and social class of parent (as defined by occupation), England and Wales, 1991–1992**

	I & II male	I & II female	IV & V male	IV & V female
All diseases	99	98	101	101
Infectious	92	88	108	112
Neoplasms	131	111	75	94
Endocrine and nutrition	89	87	91	125
Diseases of blood	79	81	102	122
Mental disorders	82	82	119	119
Nervous system	103	102	96	93
Circulatory system	117	104	90	70
Respiratory system	96	94	104	107
Digestive system	90	89	112	115
Genito-urinary system	94	86	105	115
Pregnancy	–	53	–	135
Skin diseases	94	94	104	107
Musculo-skeletal	100	88	101	110
Congenital	89	94	109	94
Signs, symptoms	93	89	113	112
Injury and poison	92	94	107	106

Note: Study population = 100.

Source: OPCS, 1995.[20]

RESPIRATORY ILLNESS

Respiratory disease accounts for a significant proportion of reported chronic illness and is by far the most common reason why young people consult their GP (see Table 2.5). Consultation rates for respiratory disease among children aged 0–15 show a social class gradient (see Table 2.4). Respiratory disorders were the most common cause of admission to hospital for 5–14 year olds in England in 1990–1991. The rate for males was 15.7 per 1,000 population, and that for females was 11.2 per 1,000 population.[14] Data from the 1946 birth cohort suggest that poor home environment, parental bronchitis, atmospheric pollution, childhood lower respiratory illness and later smoking were the best predictors of adult lower respiratory tract problems.[21] Evidence from the 1970 birth cohort suggests that children living in damp housing were more likely to have bronchitis, to wheeze and to miss school than those living in drier conditions.

All of these risks increased with the degree of severity of the dampness of their home.[5]

TABLE 2.5: **GP consultations: patient consulting rates per 1,000 persons, 15–24 year olds, England and Wales, 1981–1982 and 1991–1992**

	15–24 years (1981–1982)	16–24 years (1991–1992)
All diseases	705.4	757.2
Respiratory system	259.4	312.0
Infective and parasitic	129.7	160.2
Nervous system	94.9	106.7
Skin diseases	146.8	169.7
Injury and poisoning	134.8	151.8
Signs, symptoms	134.3	124.6
Musculo-skeletal	82.0	84.2
Genito-urinary	111.8	127.9
Digestive system	55.2	63.2
Mental disorders	63.7	61.1
Neoplasms	5.2	13.3
Congenital	1.8	3.3
Diseases of blood	4.5	5.5
Endocrine and nutrition	16.3	12.0
Circulatory system	12.4	14.6
Pregnancy	20.6	24.7

Source: *On the State of the Public Health*, 1993.

ASTHMA

Asthma is the most common chronic disease among children and young people. There remains an absence of current national prevalence figures for childhood asthma in Great Britain,[22] but prevalence is estimated to lie in the range of 10–15 per cent.[22, 23] Cumulative prevalence rates for children under 15 are estimated to be between 17 per cent and 23 per cent.[23, 24] The relationship with social class is not clear. It may be that early exposure to respiratory infection protects against asthma and this would mean that it was less commonly associated with poverty; on the other hand, untreated respiratory infections, which are more common with poverty, can precipitate asthma attacks. More research is required to investigate the relationship between asthma and environmental pollution. There is also some evidence that asthma may be underdiagnosed in young people in inner cities and in minority ethnic groups. A retrospective study conducted in a London inner-city general practice, containing large Asian and Afro-Caribbean minority populations, found the cumulative, lifetime prevalence of asthma or wheezing illness to be 19.5 per cent in children aged 15 years or under.[24]

KEY MESSAGE

Respiratory problems are more common in young people living in inner cities and those from minority ethnic groups.

DIABETES

Controversy remains about whether there is a social gradient for insulin dependent diabetes mellitus (IDDM), which usually starts in childhood or adolescence. A Scottish study that examined standard-ised hospital discharge rates for IDDM noted that children in deprived areas had an 80 per cent lower risk after adjustment for urban-rural differences.[25] Similarly, a study from Montreal, Canada, found that incidence rates for IDDM increased from 6.4 per 100,000 per year for the lowest income fifth up to 10.2 per 100,000 per year in the highest income fifth.[26] However, a case control study from Sweden found that IDDM cases were more likely to have fathers who were manual workers.[27]

The EURODIAB IDDM study was able to examine complication rates for IDDM patients across 31 European clinics.[28] Because social class is a problematic measure across different countries, education was used as the measure of socioeconomic status. It was found that patients with only primary education had worse control of their sugar levels (HbA_{1c}), higher cholesterol levels, and more damage to their eyes (retinopathy) and kidneys (nephropathy) compared to college-educated patients. A study based in Middlesbrough also found that diabetics from poorer areas were less likely to be taking insulin therapy, more likely to smoke, have other cardiovascular risk factors and worse control of their blood sugars.[29, 30] These data support the need for better education and management of diabetics, including young people from poorer circumstances, if we are to prevent the higher complication and mortality rates seen in these patients.

KEY MESSAGES

The relationship between social class and incidence of diabetes is unclear.

Poverty affects the management of diabetes.

MENTAL ILL HEALTH

UNEMPLOYMENT AND MENTAL HEALTH

Unemployment is an important risk factor for mental health problems.[31] Unemployment rates have been found to be strongly correlated with psychiatric admission rates.[32] Financial problems resulting from unemployment are an important cause of mental health problems, but a more important reason may be the effects of losing the non-financial benefits that work provides. Most of these are due to a '... loss of status, purpose and social contacts, and a time structure to the day'.[33]

Differences in mental health between unemployed and employed populations have consistently been shown. A study of young women aged 15–20 showed that the rate of self-reported mood disturbance among the unemployed girls was significantly higher than the rate among the employed.[34] These differences have also been shown to emerge among young people entering the labour market when no differences existed at school.[31]

The risk of insecure and unsatisfactory jobs can be just as depressing as unemployment itself.[31, 34] According to a survey by ChildLine, entitled *Stressed Out*, the mounting pressure for academic success and the looming spectre of youth unemployment has made schoolwork the main worry in children's lives. It also pointed out that children as young as seven are so stressed by school work and exams that some of them consider suicide.

MENTAL HEALTH AND HOMELESSNESS

Mental health problems are also closely tied in with financial worries and the consequences of living in poor housing. More and more families in the UK, particularly single-parent families, are being housed in homeless family accommodation or in B&B establishments.[35] Young people in these families have been found to be at major risk of health and behaviour problems.

Shelter suggests that there are at least 80,000 single homeless people under 25 in England and Wales.[35] Between one-third and a half are likely to have a serious mental disorder. Up to one-third of homeless people in this age group come directly from care facilities.[35] Depression, anxiety and emotional disorders are all common among homeless people but few require the services of the specialist mental health services and '...where they do, these services are best provided in the least stigmatising way possible, from the local community mental health service'.[36] Although disorders may be a cause or a consequence of homelessness, there seems little doubt that mental illness tends to get worse as homelessness continues.[35] More than half of homeless people have no idea where to seek help or advice.[35] As well as the actual lack of housing, these individuals have to endure social marginalisation.[35]

SCOPE OF MENTAL DISORDERS

It has been estimated that psychiatric disorders or handicapping abnormalities of emotions, behaviour or relationships are present in a substantial proportion (10–20 per cent) of children and young people in the general population.[37] Three broad types of stressor have been associated with mental health problems in this age group:[38]

- Normal or generic stresses – an example is moving to a new school.
- Severe acute stress – an example is parental divorce.
- Severe chronic stress – an example is poverty.

Mental health is generally assumed to cover a wide range of problems including suicide, depression and schizophrenia. However, mental health should be thought of as being more than simply the absence of mental illness.[39] This is particularly significant for young people whose state of mental health is essentially dependent on their emotional wellbeing, which is often dependent on 'the realm of interpersonal relationships and the social environment rather than having their origins in medical or cognitive factors' (Mary Lightfoot, a Social Worker in Croydon, in *Young Minds* newsletter, issue 23, October 1995). Mental health must also be considered within the cultural context because each culture has its own ideas about ideal states of mind or wellbeing.[39]

A recent report by Rutter and Smith argues that a combination of a more insular youth culture (more reliance on the influence of the peer group and less on adults) together with a movement towards more individualistic values over the last 50 years has generated a huge increase in psychosocial problems among young people.[40]

The true extent of mental health problems is not known because cases often do not come to the notice of professional agencies and so the majority of children are not under the care of psychiatric services.[37] There is also a complex interrelationship between mental health and other risk factors such as substance abuse and sexual abuse. There is relatively little information on mental health problems among minority ethnic groups, although there is some evidence of particular problems among young Asian people, who now seem to be more prone to self-harm behaviour than their white contemporaries (Joseph Aros Atolagbe, *Young Minds* newsletter, issue 16, December 1993). Recent studies show that rates of self-harm behaviour for young married Asian women are rising far more quickly than those for the white population of a similar age group. Moreover, the levels of completed suicide amongst Asian women between the ages of 15 and 24 is 80 per cent higher than for white women of the same age.[41] Mental health services in the UK have emerged '…within a largely white, Westernised culture with its own characteristic notions of health and disease'.[36] Thus, despite having higher hospital admission rates for treatment of mental disorder, and being more likely than white people to be diagnosed as having schizophrenia, people from minority ethnic groups often find it difficult to use the relevant mental health services. This is likely to be due to a variety of reasons, most notably that '…black people find the existing services difficult to approach, hard to get access to and overwhelmingly dominated by middle-class white professionals who know little of black culture'.[36]

DEPRESSION

> It felt as if everything was darkness and full of nothing, stretching out to the horizon and filling every corner. (Anna, 14 years[42])

Some mental health problems will be experienced by 10–20 per cent of young people in any one year, although the majority will not need specialist professional help.[43] The prevalence of depression rises during childhood and young adulthood and major depression is found in between 2 and 8 per cent and particularly among females. It is not uncommon for young people with depressive disorders to have co-morbid conduct and/or anxiety disorder,[37] which may conceal their depression.[44] It is important to distinguish between depression, which we all suffer from at some point in our lives, and clinical depression which is a persistent and often devastating disorder.

Depression tends to be particularly hard to diagnose among young men. Indeed, it has been estimated that underdiagnosis in men may be as high as 65 per cent.[45] Depressed young women tend to be referred to a psychiatrist more quickly than depressed young men, mainly due to the emotional problems being clear in the form of their response, whereas young men often try to alleviate their unhappiness by behaving badly.

Parental depression, particularly on the maternal side, has been consistently linked to depression in children.[34] Environmental factors outside the family, such as friendship difficulties and bullying, are also likely to be relevant factors in increasing depressive disorders among young people.[44]

As well as being affected by poverty, unemployment and other adverse social circumstances, young people are also highly susceptible to the impact of family events. Family poverty, parental unemployment, psychiatric disorder in parents, and physical and emotional neglect have consistently been shown to have a negative influence on child development and increase the risks of psychiatric (particularly conduct) disorder.[46] Furthermore, these powerful influences have been shown to repeat themselves in many families from one generation to the next.[46, 47] A US study of 14–17 year olds demonstrates the central role of economic hardship in linking family status with depression, partly through the greater vulnerability of youths in single parent families to financial stresses.[48]

The mood disturbances experienced by some young people may be carried forward into adulthood. For others, it may represent the traumas associated with growing up. However, depressive disorders that arise in childhood or early adolescence constitute a substantial psychiatric problem.[49] For a small minority, these may be the first symptoms of longer-term or more serious psychiatric illness. There is increasing evidence that depressive disorders often begin in late childhood and adolescence,[34] and that they have a high rate of recurrence into adulthood.[49] For depressive disorders, an equal sex ratio seems to exist during childhood, whereas, in both young adulthood and adulthood, women sufferers outnumber men by two or three to one.[34] Serious depression is infrequent among the young.[44] However, cases of severe depression have a high risk of recurrence extending into adult life,[49] as well as there being an increased risk of both attempted and completed suicide.[44]

Research in the London borough of Islington looked at factors in early life which contributed to depression among working-class mothers. The factors that were most significantly associated in this population were neglect, and physical and sexual abuse before the age of 17.[50] Such experiences approximately doubled the rate of adult depression, with the rate being highest among those who had suffered sexual abuse. Other research by this group has found similar patterns among young males, particularly after suffering neglect and physical abuse.

KEY MESSAGE

Depression in young people is common as a reaction to adverse circumstances.

SCHIZOPHRENIA

Schizophrenia is the most common form of severe mental illness. It affects only a small proportion of the adult population (about 1 per cent), but it is a very debilitating illness which usually begins in early adult life between the late teens and mid-twenties, often after a perfectly normal childhood.[36] Like depression, it has links with suicide, with between 10 and 12 per cent of schizophrenics committing suicide over the course of their lifetime. Even this high figure is likely to be an underestimate due to the reluctance of coroners in many instances to put down the verdict of suicide.[51] Studies of patients with schizophrenia suggest that those most at risk of suicide are young men with a short illness, a history of parasuicide, features of affective disorder, and hopelessness because of unemployment or loneliness.[52]

Schizophrenia is very strongly linked to social class, with people labelled 'working class' being five times more likely than those in other classes to be diagnosed as schizophrenic.[53] However, it has proved difficult to establish the direction of causality between social class and schizophrenia, since early symptoms may lead to educational and work failures and a drift into low occupational or residential socioeconomic groupings.[54] The relatively high prevalence among young Black people is particularly worrying.[36] In 1981, the age-standardised admission rate for Caribbean-born people aged 16+ for schizophrenia and paranoia per 100,000 population in England was three times higher among males and twice as high among females as their British-born counterparts.[55]

KEY MESSAGE

Schizophrenia is more common in poverty, and among young Black people.

SUICIDE

In 1994, 77 young people in England and Wales died as a result of suicide, self-inflicted injury and 'undetermined causes' (see Table 2.6). Despite these figures, suicide still remains a taboo subject, especially among those who are most likely to be at greatest risk.[56]

The suicide rate among young men is of particular concern, having doubled since 1975.[13] This is against the trends in other age groups.[57] Youth suicide in the UK has increased at a greater rate compared to that in other EC countries.[58] Despite young women suffering a higher incidence of both depression and parasuicide (attempted suicide), the rate of suicide is comparatively low compared to young males and has changed very little since 1980.

TABLE 2.6: **Deaths from suicide and 'undetermined causes' among 10—19 year olds, England and Wales, 1994**

	10–14 yrs	15–19 yrs
Males	13	129
Females	9	26

Source: OPCS, *Mortality Statistics – Injury and Poisoning – England and Wales*, OPCS, 1991.

The situation is likely to be even more serious because many deaths are given an open verdict, a large number of which are undoubtedly either homicide or suicide.[59] These are officially recorded as 'undetermined deaths' which increased by 100 per cent between 1980 and 1992.[60]

the recent increase in rates among young people has been greatest in deprived areas ... by 1991–93 suicide rates in young men and women living in deprived areas were about twice the rates of those living in affluent areas.[61]

Many of the geographical variations in both suicide and parasuicide rates can be accounted for by socioeconomic deprivation, so that areas with poorer individuals, as illustrated in Table 2.7, show higher rates.[32,61] Risk of death due to suicide and possible suicide was found to be 2.7 times higher for 15–24 year olds in social class V compared to the other social classes combined.[62] Low socioeconomic position has also been associated with greatly increased risk of parasuicide.[62]

TABLE 2.7: **Suicide rates per 100,000 population by sex, age, deprivation category, and year**

	Year	Affluent	Deprived
Men aged 15–29	1981-83	14.1 (43)	23.0 (84)
Men aged 15–29	1991-93	20.4 (67)	48.7 (193)
Women aged 15–29	1981-83	2.7 (8)	6.8 (23)
Women aged 15–29	1991-93	6.8 (21)	13.2 (53)

Note: Values in parentheses are numbers of deaths.

Source: McLoone, *BMJ*, 1996.[61]

Unemployment is a potentially important contributor to suicide.[62] Six per cent of deaths from suicide occur in the unemployed population.[63] Unemployment increases the likelihood of other adverse life events and lessens the psychological and social resources needed to cope with these.[31] The sense of hopelessness associated with chronic unemployment must act as a further adverse factor conducive to suicide.[64]

Where the 'unoccupied' population has been considered separately, suicide rates are found to be higher than among those in work.[64] These factors may help to explain the disproportionate rise in suicides among young men as poverty, unemployment and homelessness have affected young males more than their female counterparts.[65] The importance of the underlying social processes in affecting suicide rates was noted as far back as the 19th century by Durkheim, who suggested that many suicides in modern society could be explained by a reduction in the social integration of some groups in society, together with poverty and losses, feelings of isolation, and loss of community life. This may help explain the rise in youth suicide rates in today's society which seems to have become even more individualistic.[66]

Mental illness, such as depression and schizophrenia, constitute major risk factors for suicide but the rise in suicide rates has not been matched by a recognised increase in the prevalence of mental illness.[67] The release of mentally-ill patients into the community, without careful supervision and assessment, could have contributed to this increase.[67] Patients are at greatly increased risk of suicide shortly after discharge from psychiatric patient care.[68] It has been estimated that 50 per cent of people who commit suicide were current or former psychiatric patients and that patients within four weeks of discharge from psychiatric hospitals could represent 10–15 per cent of all suicides.[57]

Substance misuse is another major risk factor. People who misuse drugs and alcohol are 20 times more likely to commit suicide than those who do not, and alcoholics may represent 15–25 per cent of all suicides.[57] Dependence on drugs and alcohol is most common in young men aged 16–24 where it has been estimated as being as high as 17 per cent,[56] and furthermore, among young men, remaining single or getting divorced may make a substantial contribution to population suicide rates.[67]

Young men in prison aged 15–24 are six times more likely to kill themselves than their peers outside prison. These trends account for about 5 per cent of the increase in suicides among young men.[57] Many of these have a history of mental disorders and the majority involve young male remand prisoners.[36, 68] AIDS does not seem to be an important factor in the rise in the suicide rate in this age group, although the relatively small number of individuals with AIDS are at increased risk of suicide. HIV/AIDS has been estimated as accounting for 1–2 per cent of all suicides.[57]

KEY MESSAGE

Suicide, particularly related to unemployment, is an increasing problem in young men.

ATTEMPTED SUICIDE

Attempted suicide is three times more common in young women than their male counterparts.[69,70] However, the difference is narrowing as the rate is growing faster among young males. In attempted cases, relationship difficulties appear to be the most frequently quoted problem,[71] with unemployment and substance abuse also being common, especially in males.[59] Those who have attempted suicide are at least 100 times more at risk of eventually dying by suicide than the rest of the population.[56] From a public health viewpoint, '...it seems that the size of this problem [attempted suicide] in teenagers in the UK is greater than in almost any other country in Europe'.[60]

Applying the rates for deliberate self-poisoning and self-injury among young people in Oxford suggests a total of 18,000–19,000 hospital-referred cases per year in England and Wales [72] This is the most common reason for acute medical admission of young people.[60] The Oxford study indicates an increasing trend in deliberate self-harm among young people.[71] Deliberate self-harm becomes increasingly common from 12 years of age, remaining more widespread among girls.[71] Reasons for the sex difference may include earlier puberty in girls, young girls facing more problems at this age than their male counterparts and the behaviour being more acceptable to girls. Boys are also seen to have other means of expressing emotional problems, including aggressive behaviour and delinquency.[71] A substantial proportion of these young people, especially the males, were living alone or in no fixed abode, and had a history of violence or a criminal record.

Population-based epidemiological surveys of deliberate self-harm exclude homeless people and do not represent them in their conclusions. However, '...deliberate self harm in the homeless is commonly seen in inner city hospitals and the homeless are probably at higher risk of eventual suicide'.[72] A study of all patients aged 16 and over who presented to an inner London hospital after an episode of deliberate self-harm during a three-year period showed that 15 per cent of patients were of no fixed abode.[72]

KEY MESSAGE

Attempted suicide in young people is also strongly related to poverty.

EATING DISORDERS

Eating disorders are generally classified into two groups of conditions, anorexia nervosa and bulimia nervosa. This oversimplifies the picture, as some individuals may have features of both conditions and many more may have abnormal attitudes or behaviours towards eating, as measured by questionnaire, yet will not formally be diagnosed as having any eating disorder.

Anorexia nervosa is a rare disorder, although it can be fatal or persistent for many years with a relatively high level of morbidity. Most data on the incidence of anorexia nervosa originate from hospital data, and are therefore limited to more severe cases. Perhaps the best epidemiologically-based data come from a Dutch primary care morbidity survey, which reported incidence rates of 6.3 per 100,000.[73] There is some debate as to whether there has been an actual increase in anorexia rates or whether there is now simply better diagnosis and case ascertainment. Prevalence rates are obviously higher: one study has noted a one-year prevalence of 0.16 per cent for females aged 15–29 in primary care while another found a prevalence of 0.48 per cent for girls aged 15–19 in Rochester, Minnesota.[74]

Bulimia is a relatively new diagnosis with a better prognosis than anorexia.[75] It is far more common than anorexia, and women suffering from it are more likely to be able to maintain personal relationships and work. The incidence rates for bulimia in the Dutch primary care system were noted to be 11.4 per 100,000 per year during 1985–1989,[73] although this is likely to be a gross underestimate of the problem: because of 'the greater taboo around bulimia nervosa and its smaller perceptibility compared to anorexia nervosa, the true incidence rate of bulimia nervosa seems still as much a secret as the syndrome itself.' Far better data exist for the prevalence of bulimia, the prevalence rate being around 1 per cent among adolescent and young women, though this still may be an underestimate as individuals with eating disorders may be overrepresented among subjects unwilling to take part in a research study.[76]

All studies show that men are far less likely to develop eating disorders than women: only 7 per cent of the anorectics were male and 4 per cent of bulimics.[73] The social class distribution of eating disorders is less clear and most studies tend to report greater prevalence rates among the middle and upper classes. Mean scores on the EAT questionnaire, which measures eating problems, were greater for state rather than private schools, but the number of anorexia cases was greater in the private schools.[77] This may reflect sociocultural differences in the acceptability and presentation of psychopathology. Girls from poorer homes maintain normal weight or may be obese but binge, while those from richer homes chose to restrict food consumption, thus becoming excessively thin. Class itself may bias the likelihood of both being ascertained and diagnosed as having an eating disorder.[78]

A recent prospective study investigating self-esteem in young women aged 11–12, who were then followed up at 15–16, revealed that those with low self-esteem were at far greater risk of developing eating disorders than their peers who had a positive self-image. This research also argues that eating disorders 'are multifactorally determined'. Five hundred and ninety-four young women were initially interviewed and approximately 400 of these were followed up at 15–16. About 60 per cent of the interviewees were from households classified as social class I or II, with 40 per cent from lower socioeconomic backgrounds. The researchers found that lower social class '... predicted lower self-esteem and depressive symptoms'. Low self-esteem respondents were eight times more likely to develop eating disorders. Influences which seemed to have the greatest effect on self-esteem in these young women were:

- social conditions;
- home environment;
- symptoms of depression; and
- problems at school.

All four of these are affected by both poverty and affluence.

Body image, concerns with weight and dieting are usually associated with young women, but a recent survey of 3,500 young people in Scotland, aged between 11 and 16, found that 'looks and weight were among the causes of concern ... to boys as well as girls, and almost 1 in 10 overall said they were dieting'. But being diet conscious does not inevitably lead to eating disorders: young people with diabetes have to be very careful both about their weight and diet but yet are no more at risk of eating disorders. This, it is suggested, may be due to the young person's awareness of the effect anorexia or bulimia could have on their health, or, because of the supervision of parents and medical practitioners.

KEY MESSAGE

Some eating disorders are associated with the low self-esteem resulting from poverty in young people.

HIV/AIDS AND PREGNANCY IN YOUNG PEOPLE

HIV/AIDS

In the *Health of the Nation* document HIV/AIDS is referred to as one of the greatest threats to public health this century. HIV/AIDS is seen as a disease of the 1980s and '90s and, therefore, frequently associated with sexually active young people. However, some research suggests that younger people are more responsible regarding the use of condoms as a protection against HIV than are 45–54 year olds.[79] However, the responses given by young people in surveys on sexual attitudes and behaviours may be influenced by their beliefs regarding interviewers' 'moral judgements', and fears about confidentiality and under-age sex. But most generalisations regarding the attitudes of young people to sexual health exclude, more often than not, the young people who are most at risk – those who sell sex, and the homeless.

Current trends in HIV/AIDS-related behaviour among young people indicate that:

9% of people who are HIV positive are in the 15-19 age group;

young men who leave school early '… become less positive about using condoms';[80]

young people say that they would like more holistic sex education which includes emotional and psychological aspects of sexuality, sexual identity and HIV;[81]

over one-third of young people interviewed for *Health Promotion Wales* (1995)[82] were too embarrassed to consult their GPs about sexual health and an additional third were concerned about confidentiality;

young people in rural areas often find it difficult to buy condoms anonymously;[80]

women with AIDS are proportionately more likely to be younger. 22% of cases among women are in the under 25s;

the number of cases of HIV infection is much higher among young men compared to young women; and

there is a relationship between sexual activity under the age of 16 and higher rates of STDs.

Sources: [83-85]

But sexual health includes more than sexually transmitted diseases (STDs). It comprises family planning, pregnancy and advisory services and, in its most positive sense, it is a '... measure of physical/ psychological wellbeing'. Nevertheless, take-up of any health service or clinic specifically designed to meet the needs of young people is, to a great extent, dependent on knowledge, access to services and, one of the most important factors for young people, confidentiality.

KEY MESSAGE

Sexually transmitted diseases, including HIV/AIDS, are associated with poverty in young people.

YOUNG PEOPLE, PREGNANCY AND POVERTY

'Districts with high underprivileged area scores were more likely to have high rates of conception among teenagers'.[86]

Teenage mothers are more likely to have left school early, come from lower socioeconomic households and, if they have a termination, are more likely to have a late abortion than women over 20. There has been a decline in under-16 conceptions since 1990, but UK teenage conceptions are nearly five times the rate of the Netherlands (see Table 2.8).

Although there has been a small decline in pregnancies among young people in the UK there is no cause for complacency as seen from the international comparisons in Table 2.8. Although other countries had higher rates than the UK (not shown) the many countries with lower rates demonstrate what could be done. Many of the high numbers of teenage births may be attributable to poor access to family planning services and, as seen in one study, only 29.1 per cent of pregnancies were terminated in the most deprived areas compared to 62.2 per cent terminations in the most affluent.[86] Nor are all young people aware of their rights to confidentiality and treatment. The Royal College of Physicians (1995) refer to young people's '... particular concerns about confidentiality and fear that this will not always be respected by general practitioners or family planning clinics'.[87] This may be a major factor contributing to the lower utilisation of family planning clinics and preventative health services by the poorest in society.[88] A lack of confidence in health professionals and sense of non-confidentiality can further affect young women's sexual and reproductive health. For example, over 50 per cent of young people interviewed for Health Promotion Wales in 1995 thought that GPs had to get parental consent before giving contraceptive advice.

TABLE 2.8: **Number of births per 1,000 women aged 15–19, worldwide, 1990–1995**

Country	Fertility rate
Japan	4
Switzerland	5
The Netherlands	7
France	9
Italy	9
Belgium	10
Denmark	10
Malta	12
Spain	12
Finland	13
Germany	13
Luxembourg	13
Sweden	13
Albania	14
Ireland	16
Norway	19
Israel	20
Australia	21
Greece	22
Austria	23
Portugal	25
Canada	27
Belarus	28
Poland	28
Iceland	29
Slovenia	30
Croatia	32
Lithuania	32
Bosnia/Hercegovina	33
United Kingdom	**33**

Source: *The Progress of Nations*, UNICEF, 1996.

In *Health of the Nation*,[89] diet is referred to as an area where '... there is a clear scope for improving the health of pregnant women, infants and children' and in reducing '... preventable death and ill-health among pregnant women, infants and children'. Yet healthy eating as a proactive health measure appears to be constrained by poverty. An inner-city GP recently commented that making healthy eating recommendations to young mothers living in poverty, who could thus afford little improvement in their diet, was the equivalent of 'pissing in the wind'.

Dietary deficiencies in pregnant young women

As many as 1 in 4 young women between 14-18 appear to consume 'totally inadequate' amounts of calcium.

Maximum bone mass is not reached until the end of adolescence 'just before the child-bearing period'.

Anaemic and iron-deficient infants are not exceptional in areas with high deprivation scores.

Young women's diets are more likely to be poor where there is a concentration of social housing.

The most important factor influencing women's diet is low income.[90, 91]

KEY MESSAGES

Teenage pregnancies are more common in disadvantaged young people.

These young mothers are at risk of dietary deficiencies.

SUBSTANCE ABUSE AND POVERTY IN YOUNG PEOPLE

SMOKING

In the National Audit Commission's recent progress report on Health of the Nation it is stated that targets for smoking in young people have not been met, in fact rates appear to be rising, as Figure 2.3 shows.

The trend among older teenagers is of concern. In 1990, 30 per cent of young people in Britain aged 16-19 were smokers.[4] Again, the prevalence is higher among females, with 32 per cent smoking compared to 28 per cent of males. A recent survey of 7,722 pupils in the UK aged 15–16 found that two-thirds had smoked cigarettes at some time, over one-third had smoked in the past 30 days, and about 6 per cent had smoked more than 10 cigarettes per day in the past 30 days.[92]

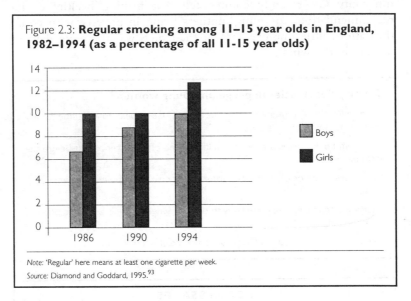

Figure 2.3: **Regular smoking among 11–15 year olds in England, 1982–1994 (as a percentage of all 11-15 year olds)**

Note: 'Regular' here means at least one cigarette per week.
Source: Diamond and Goddard, 1995.[93]

Rates of smoking vary between different social groups, with children from lower social groups smoking more than those in higher classes.[4]

Recent data show that by the late teenage years, the '… prevalence of smoking is highest amongst semi-skilled and unskilled manual groups'.[4] Also, a cohort study of young people and their parents in the West of Scotland found social class to be independently associated with young people's smoking, with young people from lower social class households being most likely to smoke.[94] Smoking has also been related to other markers of socioeconomic position, namely lone parent status, housing tenure, and employment status.[95] Parental influence is also an important factor in whether or not young people smoke, so strong social class gradients in adult smoking rates are likely to have a stronger influence on young people starting, or continuing to smoke.

A potentially strong influence that may help to explain these trends in older smokers is the working environment. Young people from poorer socioeconomic backgrounds might not have the resources to be able to afford to smoke much when they are still at school, but when they start work, although it may be on low pay, they can afford to buy at least a limited number of cigarettes each week. This is a possible explanation as to why social class differences begin to show up from early adulthood. Also, these groups tend to go into jobs which are low paid and have a more 'working-class' ethos and so smoking in the workplace may be more acceptable.

The prevalence of smoking among young minority ethnic groups is generally lower than among the white population. Much of this is related to the different cultural norms regarding smoking behaviour. For example, among young people of Asian origin, it is deemed disrespectful to smoke in front of older members of the family.[96] However, there is some evidence that smoking is becoming more acceptable to certain groups of Asian males as their attitudes and behavioural norms shift towards their country of settlement.[97]

TABLE 2.9: **Percentage of teenagers aged 15 who smoke every day, worldwide, 1993–1994**

Country	Males	Females
Israel	6	5
Lithuania	9	2
Slovakia	13	3
Czech Republic	11	6
Russian Federation	13	5
Estonia	16	3
United States	10	10
Sweden	10	13
Poland	17	8
Denmark	10	17
Norway	16	15
Hungary	19	13
Belgium	19	14
Spain	15	19
Germany	16	19
France	18	18
Canada	16	21
Scotland	**17**	**21**
Northern Ireland	**20**	**20**
Austria	21	21
Finland	25	19

Source: The Progress of Nations, UNICEF, 1996.

Table 2.9 show how badly Scotland and Ireland are faring in the percentage of 15 year olds who smoke every day, compared with some other countries. The table includes all countries for which data were presented by UNICEF – England was not among these.

ALCOHOL

Among young people alcohol is the drug most commonly used at both legal and illegal ages.[98] Regular drinking often starts at an early age – 20 per cent of 9–15 year olds have had their first alcoholic drink by the age of 8, and 89 per cent by 13. By the age of 15 or 16, 94 per cent of young people have consumed alcohol on at least one occasion.[89] Among those who had not, the main reason was religious beliefs.[92] Most 15–16 year olds (78 per cent) had at some point experienced intoxication.[92] Boys tend to start drinking at an earlier age and drink more often and in larger quantities than girls. A Health Education Authority survey in 1992 showed that, among 11–15 year olds who drank in the preceding week, 5 per cent of girls and 3 per cent of boys exceeded the recommended limits for adults.

The 1992 HEA Survey suggests small social class differences in drinking among young people. Among 9–15 year olds those from professional backgrounds tend to drink slightly less. These differences converge for those aged 16–19. The West of Scotland cohort study found that young people from non-manual households were more likely to drink than those living in manual households.[94] It may be that social class differences again develop during late teenage years and early adulthood, for many of the same reasons as they develop among regular smokers.

Alcohol abuse among young people is often linked to poor scholastic achievement, school-based problem behaviour, truancy, unemployment, delinquency and relationship problems.[99] Young people who feel excluded from society, such as lone parents and the unemployed, are more likely to drink heavily than those who are more socially integrated. Unemployment of six months or more in total has been significantly associated with heavier drinking in young men, even after allowing for drinking patterns at age 16.[100] On the other hand, those with more money in their pockets can afford to spend more on alcohol.

Most young people begin to drink alcohol in the home, in the company of parents and other family members. The relationship between parental drinking and the drinking habits of their children is not always clear cut because the literature has tended to focus on problem drinking rather than drinking *per se*.[94] However, several studies show that parental influence is usually an important factor in the drinking habits of their children, although the relationship is complicated.[94] Evidence from both the National Child Development Study and the West of Scotland Cohort study suggests that young people in non-manual families are more likely to drink with their parents, either at home or in restaurants. Young people who only mentioned drinking in pubs at 16 were more likely to be in the heavy drinking category at age 23 than those who only drank at home at age 16. Thus Green, *et al.*, based on the findings from these studies, make the tentative conclusion that '...an early introduction to alcohol within the family home is less likely to lead to problem drinking'.[94]

KEY MESSAGE

Poor young people are more likely to misuse tobacco in the transition to adulthood.

HOW POVERTY AFFECTS DRUG TAKING IN YOUNG PEOPLE

The main reasons for young people's taking drugs are similar to those outlined for alcohol and cigarette smoking and include: boredom and stress; rebellion; coping strategy against poverty and its related problems; enjoyment; and peer influence. Drugs are often taken as a means of trying to alleviate the effects of poverty and social deprivation. It seems that '... illegal drug use is higher in young people from single parent families ... [and] in families where there is already someone into illegal drug use'.[98] Experimentation with illegal drugs does not appear to vary much between social groups, but addiction and regular use are more likely to develop among young people from lower social classes.[101] Indeed, 'experimentation is seen across all social classes, but at the compulsive user end there are many more people from poor and socially deprived back-grounds'.[98] A study of drug misuse in Liverpool involving opiates and cocaine found a strong correlation between the number of known drug users per 1,000 population in each electoral ward and material deprivation and unemployment rates.[102] Heavy drug use is commonly linked to crime and violence, often through the need to steal or actually deal in drugs in order to feed the habit. For some it is a downward spiral from which it is almost impossible to escape, leading to homelessness, drug dealing, and prostitution.

Why take drugs?

Around here, it doesn't take much to realise why they start either. Out of 165 school leavers last year at the local school, two got jobs after six months. In such an environment, you don't have to do much promoting as a dealer to make your drugs tempting. It's just a cheap mental breakout from a very depressing situation. There are a lot of people out there kicking around with nothing to do … drugs are the perfect answer – artificial fun (John, drug counsellor from South London).[98]

But it may be just to get away from harsh circumstances in general. It's another way of escape isn't it? If you come from a more secure background, it mightn't stop you experimenting, but you might not need it so badly – the escape bit that is (Guy, a 20 year-old university student).[98]

KEY MESSAGE

Poverty induces serious misuse of illegal drugs in young people.

LONG-TERM EFFECTS OF POVERTY

The detrimental effects of their environment on the health status of young people in severe poverty, and homeless young people in particular, is self-evident and difficult to deny. The more general issue of socioeconomic inequalities in health among young people outside these extreme groups is less obvious. Youth is a period generally characterised by the best health people ever have throughout their lives. This is reflected in its also being the period with the lowest mortality rates. Some authors have considered that inequalities in health are characterised more by their absence than their presence at this age.[103] However, socioeconomic differences are seen in precisely those aspects of health status which have the most important long-term influences. It is becoming increasingly apparent that the risk of many important illnesses in adulthood is influenced by what happens in earlier life. Low birthweight has been shown to be related to increased coronary heart disease, stroke and respiratory disease mortality, showing that one of the earliest characteristics of an individual can influence what happens later in their life. Birthweight remains strongly related to social position in Britain, reinforcing the fact that people in different social groups are born with different life chances.

Children in less favourable socioeconomic circumstances are shorter than their peers and this height difference translates into sizeable differences in the risk of morbidity and mortality from many common diseases in later life. Similarly the children of poor mothers are more likely to be iron deficient, which has consequences for long-term development. Respiratory function and the presence of respiratory symptoms in childhood, which presage the development of respiratory disease in later life, also indicate that what happens in childhood is of particular importance for adult health. Social class differences in smoking behaviour, which begin to emerge at the end of the age period under consideration, will in time be translated into large differences in health and the risk of premature death.

Health and concerns about long-term health issues such as preventing heart disease in later life can be a low priority for young people who are poor. For these people the most important issues include housing and job security, their range of choices for the future, and the presence of supportive social networks – all of which contribute to their mental, physical and psychological wellbeing. Understanding the influences of social inequality on the quality of life of young people requires an approach which embraces the full spectrum of their experiences including many which lie outside those conventionally considered important for health.

SUMMARY

The main messages about health problems in young people, which are associated with poverty, are:

- young people in poverty suffer more accidents causing deaths and injury;
- respiratory problems are more common in young people living in inner cities, and in those from minority ethnic groups, and there is a definite association with poverty;

- poverty affects the management of diabetes;
- depression in young people is common as a reaction to adverse circumstances;
- schizophrenia is more common in poverty, especially in young Black people;
- suicide, particularly related to unemployment, is an increasing problem in young men, while attempted suicide in young people is strongly related to poverty;
- sexually transmitted diseases, including HIV/AIDS, are associated with poverty in young people;
- teenage pregnancies are more common in disadvantaged young people, and these young mothers are at greater risk of dietary deficiencies; and
- poor young people are more likely to misuse tobacco in the transition to adulthood.

NOTES

1. C Woodroffe and M Glickman, 'Trends in child health', *Children and Society*, 1993, 7: 49-63.
2. K Judge and M Benzeval, 'Health inequalities: new concerns about the children of single mothers', *British Medical Journal*, 1993, 306: 677-80.
3. OPCS, *Mortality Statistics – Injury and Poisoning – England & Wales*, OPCS, 1991.
4. B Botting, 'A review of the health of our children, decennial supplement', *Population Trends*, 1995, 82: 27-33.
5. C Woodroffe, *Children, Teenagers and Health*, Macmillan, 1993.
6. S Jarvis, E Towner and S Walsh, 'Accidents' in B Botting (ed), *The Health of Our Children: Decennial Supplement* (Series DS No. 11), OPCS, 1995.
7. I Roberts and C Power, 'Does the decline in child injury mortality vary by social class? A comparison of class specific mortality in 1981 and 1991', *British Medical Journal*, 1996, 313: 784-6.
8. E M L Towner, S N Jarvis, S S M Walsh and A Aynsley-Green, 'Measuring exposure to injury risk in schoolchildren aged 11–14', *British Medical Journal*, 1994, 308: 449-52.
9. I Roberts, 'Why have child pedestrian death rates fallen?', *British Medical Journal*, 1993, 306: 1737-9.
10. I Roberts and B Pless, 'Social policy as a cause of childhood accidents: the children of lone mothers', *British Medical Journal*, 1996, 311: 925-8.
11. P M Sharples, A Storey, A Aynsley-Green and J A Eyre, 'Causes of fatal childhood accidents involving head injury in Northern region,

1979-86', *British Medical Journal*, 1990, 301: 1193-7.

12. G Sparks, M A Craven and C Worth, 'Understanding differences between high and low childhood accident rate areas: the importance of qualitative data', *Journal of Public Health Medicine*, 1994, 16: 439-46.

13. DoH, *Hospital Episode Statistics: Finished Consultant Episodes by Diagnosis, Operation and Speciality*, Department of Health, 1990-91.

14. S S Walsh and S N Jarvis, 'Measuring the frequency of "severe" accidental injury in childhood', *Journal of Epidemiology and Community Health*, 1992, 46: 26-32.

15. J Sibert, 'Injuries to adolescents', in A Macfarlane (ed), *Adolescent Medicine*, Royal College of Physicians, 1996.

16. M Barker and C Power, 'Disability in young adults: the role of injuries', *Journal of Epidemiology and Community Health*, 1993, 47: 349-54.

17. J P Mackenbach, W N L Caspar and B W Joost, 'Differences in the misreporting of chronic conditions, by level of education: the effect on inequalitics in prevalence rates', *American Journal of Public Health*, 1996, 86: 706-11.

18. General Household Survey, *Living in Britain: Results from the 1994 General Household Survey*, HMSO, 1994.

19. P West, G Ford, K Hunt, S Macintyre and R Ecob, 'How sick is the west of Scotland? Age specific comparisons with national datasets on a range of health measures', *Scottish Medical Journal*, 1994, 39: 101-9.

20. OPCS, *Morbidity Statistics from General Practice: Fourth National Study 1991-1992*, HMSO, 1995.

21. S L Mann, M E J Wadsworth and J R T Colley, 'Accumulation of factors influencing respiratory illness in members of a national birth cohort and their offspring', *Journal of Epidemiology and Community Health*, 1992, 46: 286-92.

22. D P Strachan, H R Anderson, E S Limb, A O'Neill and N Wells, 'A national survey of asthma prevalence, severity, and treatment in Great Britain', *Archives of Disease in Childhood*, 1994, 70: 174-8.

23. A Jones, 'Asthma remains an under-diagnosed and under-treated condition in children', *The Practitioner*, 1990, 234: 219-21.

24. A R Gellert, S L Gellert and S R Iliffe, 'Prevalence and management of asthma in a London inner city general practice', *British Journal of General Practice*, 1990, 40: 197-201.

25. C C Patterson and N R Waugh, 'Urban/rural and deprivational differences in incidence and clustering of childhood diabetes in Scotland', *International Journal of Epidemiology*, 1992, 21: 108-17.

26. E Colle, J Siemiatycki, R West, M M Belmonte, M P Crepeau and R Poirer, *et al.*, 'Incidence of juvenile onset diabetes in Montreal – demonstration of ethnic differences and socio-economic class differences', *Journal of Chronic Disease*, 1981, 34: 611-16.

27. L Blom, G Dahlquist, L Nystrom, A Sandstorm and S Wall, 'The

Swedish childhood diabetes study – social and perinatal determinants for diabetes in childhood', *Diabetolgia*, 1989, 32: 7–13.

28. N Chaturvedi, J Fuller and J M Stephenson, 'The relationship between socioeconomic status and diabetes control and complications in the EURODIAB IDDM complications study', *Diabetes Care*, 1996, 19: 423–9.

29. W F Kelly, R Mahmood, S Turner and K Elliott, 'Geographical mapping of diabetic patients from the deprived inner city shows less insulin therapy and more hyperglycaemia', *Diabetic Medicine*, 1993, 11: 344–8.

30. W F Kelly, R Mahmood, M J Kelly, S Turner and K Elliott, 'Influence of social deprivation on illness in diabetic patients', *British Medical Journal*, 1993, 307: 1115–16.

31. M Bartley, 'Unemployment and ill health: understanding the relationship', *Journal of Epidemiology and Community Health*, 1994, 48: 333–7.

32. D Gunnell, T J Peters, R M Kammerling and J Brooks, 'Relation between parasuicide, suicide, psychiatric admissions, and socioeconomic deprivation', *British Medical Journal*, 1995, 311: 226–30.

33. R Smith, 'Occupationless health: I feel really ashamed: how does unemployment lead to poorer mental health?', *British Medical Journal*, 1985, 291: 1409–13.

34. E Monck, P Graham, N Richman and R Dobbs, 'Self-reported mood disturbance in a community population', *British Journal of Psychiatry*, 1994, 165: 760–9.

35. J Scott, 'Homelessness and mental illness', *British Journal of Psychiatry*, 1993, 162: 314–24.

36. E Murphy, *After the Asylums: Community Care for People with Mental Illness*, Faber and Faber Limited, 1991.

37. J Hunter, I Higginson and E Garralda, 'Systematic literature review: outcome measures for child and adolescent mental health services', *Journal of Public Health Medicine*, 1996, 18: 197–206.

38. R Hodgson and T Abbasi, *Effective Mental Health Promotion: Literature Review*, Health Promotion, Wales, 1995.

39. P Wilson, 'Working space: a mentally healthy young nation', *Youth and Policy*, 1995, 51: 60–3.

40. M Rutter and D J Smith, *Psychosocial Disorders in Young People*, John Wiley & Sons, 1995.

41. J A Atolagbe, *Young Minds* newsletter, Issue 16, December 1993.

42. P Graham and C Hughes, *So Young, So Sad, So Listen*, Royal College of Psychiatrists, 1995.

43. H Williams, 'Health and illness in adolescents: a national overview', in *Health of the Young Nation*, DoH, 1996.

44. R Harrington, 'Depressive disorder in adolescence', *Archives of Disease*

in Childhood, 1995, 72: 193-5.

45. T Agnew, 'Male disorder', *Observer Life*, 12 May 1996.

46. I M Goodyer, 'Development psychopathology: the impact of recent life events in anxious and depressed school-age children', *Journal of the Royal Society of Medicine*, 1994, 87: 327-9.

47. A Bifulco, 'The first steps on the road to depression', *MRC News*, 1994, 24-7.

48. R H Aseltine, 'Pathways linking parental divorce with adolescent depression', *Journal of Health and Social Behaviour*, 1996, 37: 133-48.

49. R Harrington, H Fudge, M Rutter, A Pickles and J Hill, 'Adult outcomes of childhood and adolescent depression', *Archives of General Psychiatry*, 1990, 47: 465-73.

50. Medical Research Council, *MRC News*, Summer, 1996, no. 67, part 1.1.

51. National Schizophrenia Fellowship, 'A Positive Response to Mental Illness', *National Schizophrenia Fellowship Magazine*, Winter, 1996.

52. L Appleby, 'Suicide in psychiatric patients: risk and prevention', *British Journal of Psychiatry*, 1992, 161: 749-58.

53 P C L Heaven (ed), *Adolescent Health: The Role of the Individual Differences*, Routledge, 1992.

54. P B Jones, P Bebbington, A Foerster, S W Lewis, A Russell and P C Sham, *et al.*, 'Premorbid social underachievement in schizophrenia results from the Camberwell Collaborative Psychosis Study', *British Journal of Psychiatry*, 1993, 162: 65-71.

55. C Smaje, *Health Race and Ethnicity: Making Sense of the Evidence*, King's Fund Institute, 1995.

56. The Samaritans, *Challenging the Taboo: Attitudes Towards Suicide and Depression*, The Samaritans, 1996.

57. J Charlton, 'Trends and patterns in suicide in England and Wales', *International Journal of Epidemiology*, 1995, 24: 45-52.

58. C Pritchard, 'Is there a link between suicide in young men and unemployment? A comparison of the UK with other European Community countries', *British Journal of Psychiatry*, 1992, 160: 750-6.

59. A Macfarlane and A McPherson, 'From puberty to poverty – the health problems and needs of adolescents', *Current Paediatrics*, 1992, 1: 1-9.

60. K Hawton, 'Suicide and attempted suicide in young people', in A Macfarlane (ed), *Adolescent Medicine*, Royal College of Physicians, 1996.

61. P McLoone, 'Suicide and deprivation in Scotland', *British Medical Journal*, 1996, 312: 543-4.

62. K Hawton, J Fagg, S Platt and M Hawkins, 'Factors associated with suicide after parasuicide in young people', *British Medical Journal*, 1993, 306: 1641-4.

63. D Gunnell and S Frankel, 'Prevention of suicide: aspirations and evidence', *British Medical Journal*, 1994, 308: 1227-31.

64. N Kreitman, V Carstairs and J Duffy, 'Association of age and social class with suicide among men in Great Britain', *Journal of Epidemiology and Community Health*, 1991, 45: 195-202.

65. G M G McClure, 'Suicide in children and adolescents in England and Wales, 1960-1990', *British Journal of Psychiatry*, 1994, 165: 510-14.

66. D Gunnell, *The Potential for Preventing Suicide: A Review of the Literature on the Effectiveness of Interventions Aimed at Preventing Suicide*, University of Bristol, 1994.

67. J Charlton, S Kelly, K Dunnell, B Evans and R Jenkins, 'Suicide deaths in England and Wales: trends in factors associated with suicide deaths', *Population Trends*, 1993, 71: 34-42.

68. M Goldacre, V Seagroatt and K Hawton, 'Suicide after discharge from psychiatric inpatient care', *Lancet*, 1993, 42: 283-5.

69. K Hawton, J Fagg, S Simkin, E Bale and A Bond, *Attempted Suicide in Oxford*, Report, 1996.

70. K Hawton and J Fagg, 'Deliberate self-poisoning and self-injury in adolescents: a study of characteristics and trends in Oxford, 1976-89', *British Journal of Psychiatry*, 1992, 161: 816-23.

71. K Hawton, J Fagg and S Simkin, 'Deliberate self-poisoning and self - injury in children and adolescents under 16 years of age in Oxford, 1976-1993', *British Journal of Psychiatry*, 1996, 169: 202-8.

72. S Cullum, S O'Brien, A Burgess, J Booth, A Lant and J Catalan, 'Deliberate self harm: the hidden population', *Health Trends*, 1995, 27: 130-2.

73 H W Hoek, 'The incidence and prevalence of anorexia nervosa and bulimia nervosa in primary care', *Psychiatric Medicine*, 1991, 21: 455-60.

74. A R Lucas, C M Beard, W M O'Fallon and L T Kurland, '50-year trends in the incidence of anorexia nervosa in Rochester, Minn: a population-based study', *American Journal of Psychiatry*, 1991, 148: 917-22.

75. G F M Russell, 'Bulimia nervosa: an ominous variant of anorexia nervosa', *Psychiatric Medicine*, 1979, 9: 429-48.

76. C G Fairburn and S J Beglin, 'Studies of the epidemiology of bulimia nervosa', *American Journal of Psychiatry*, 1990, 147: 401-8.

77. I Esler and G I Szmukler, 'Social class as a confounding variable in the eating attitudes test', *Journal of Psychiatric Research*, 1985, 19: 171-6.

78. R Dixey, 'Healthy eating in schools and "eating disorders" – are "healthy eating" messages part of the problem or part of the solution?' in *Nutrition and Health Vol. 11*, A B Academic Publishers, 1996.

79. G Malbon, A Bridgwood, D Lader and J Matheson, *Health in England: What People Know, What People Think, What People Do*, OPCS, 1995.

80. D Abrams, P Sheeran, C Abraham and R Spears, 'Context and

content: the impact of school-leaving and school-based health education on AIDS-relevant cognitions', *Aids Care*, 1992, 4: 245-58.

81. C Few, I Hicken and T Butterworth, 'Alliances in school sex education: teachers' and school nurses' views', *Health Visitor*, 1996, 69: 220-3.

82. Health Promotion Wales, 'Sexual health of young people in Wales: findings from the 1995 Welsh Youth Health Survey', *HPW Technical Report no. 17*, 1995.

83. G Ross, 'Teenage clinics – the rough guide', *British Journal of Sexual Medicine*, 1996, 18-22.

84. E C Williams, R J E Kirkman and M Elstein, 'Profile of young people's advice clinic in reproductive health 1988-93', *British Medical Journal*, 1994, 309: 786-8.

85. R S Bucks, A Williams, M J Whitfield and D A Routh, 'Towards a typology of general practitioners' attitudes to general practice', *Social Science and Medicine*, 1990, 30: 537-47.

86. Health Promotion for Wales. *Caring for the Future*, HPAW, 1994.

87. Royal College of Physicians, *Sex Education for Young People: A Background Review*, Royal College of Physicians, 1995.

88. M Benzeval, K Judge and M Whitehead, *Tackling Inequalities in Health*, Kings Fund, 1995.

89. Department of Health, *The Health of the Nation*, HMSO, 1992.

90. National Dairy Council, *Calcium and Bone Health*, Topical Update – 7, June 1996.

91. R Rizzoli and J P Bonjour, 'Pregnancy-associated osteoporosis, *Lancet*, 1996, 347: 1274-5.

92. A Diamond and E Goddard, *Smoking Among Secondary School Children in 1994*, HMSO, 1995.

93. P McC Miller and M Plant, 'Drinking, smoking, and illicit drug use among 15 and 16 year olds in the United Kingdom', *British Medical Journal*, 1996, 313: 394-7.

94. G Green, S MacIntyre, P West and R Ecob, 'Like parent like child? Associations between drinking and smoking behaviour of parents and their children', *British Journal of Addiction*, 1991, 86: 745-58.

95. M Stead, G Hastings and C Tudor-Smith, 'Preventing adolescent smoking: a review of options', *Health Education Journal*, 1996, 55: 31-54.

96. J Brannen and P Storey, *Child Health in Social Context*, Health Education Authority, 1996.

97. L Mitchell, *Smoking Prevention Programmes for Adolescents – A Literature Review*, The National Adolescent and Student Health Unit, Oxford, 1994.

98. A Macfarlane, M Macfarlane and P Robson, *The User*, Oxford University Press, 1996.

99. Royal College of Physicians, *Alcohol and the Young*, British Paediatric Association, 1995.

100. C Power and V Estaugh, 'The role of family formation and dissolution in shaping drinking behaviour in early adulthood', *British Journal of Addiction*, 1990, 85: 521–30.

101. M Sheehan, E Oppenheimer and C Taylor, 'Who comes for treatment: drug misusers at three London agencies', *British Journal of Addiction*, 1988, 83: 311–20.

102. N F Squires, N J Beeching, B J M Schlecht and S M Ruben, 'An estimate of the prevalence of drug misuse in Liverpool and a spatial analysis of known addiction', *Journal of Public Health Medicine*, 1995, 17: 103–9.

103. P West, *et al.*, 'Social class and health in youth: findings from the west of Scotland Twenty–07 Study', *Social Science and Medicine*, 1990, 30: 665–73.

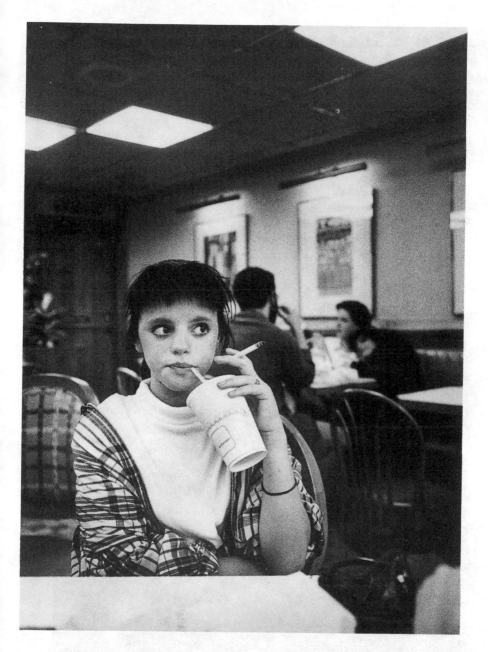

In 1990, 30 per cent of young people in Britain aged 16–19 were smokers
Credit: Monique Cabral/Format

If young people are involved in health education, they come up with different ideas from adults which are likely to be more successful

Credit: Maggie Murray/Format

3 Health-related initiatives and interventions

INTRODUCTION

Health-related initiatives and interventions for young people which have been reported have particularly focused on the areas of mental health, sexual health and drugs misuse. We have chosen to select effective or potentially effective interventions and this means, for example, that there is no specific example included for respiratory disease intervention. However, it should be noted that the consideration of providing 'user friendly' and appropriate services for young people is made with the belief that better-applied services will be better able to address the majority of common health problems.

RESEARCH AND EVALUATION

CONTROLLED STUDIES

Two recent research reviews on the effectiveness of controlled interventions to improve health in the socially disadvantaged (most recently termed 'interventions to reduce variations in health'), located just sixteen studies of interventions to improve the health of deprived young people, and only six of these were of sufficient quality to merit serious consideration.[1, 2] There are several reasons why there are so few controlled studies on health interventions for deprived young people. First, it must be seen as ethical to deny any control group the intervention. Secondly, and perhaps most relevantly for young people in poverty, the intervention must be seen as useful by those who might benefit most from it. Because of the scarcity of controlled trials, we have included some research from outside the UK, notably from the USA.

The controlled studies which have been reported are often deficient, not so much because of 'technical' problems but because the researchers have not described the processes involved in the project and how they might have affected the results. These processes need to be reflected from the point of view of both the researchers and the young people themselves. Also, the projects are often too ambitious in setting out to complete, usually within a short timescale, several complex stages of research. This does not allow sufficient time for pilot work, with the engaging of young people and their views. Another common feature is that results are reported no more than six months after the intervention with an assumption that behaviour change will be sustained. Those studies which have continued on for as long as five years have found, in the main, that the behaviour changes have not been maintained.

EVALUATIONS

Given that controlled trials may not be appropriate for all aspects of young people's health, it is important to draw on other methods, especially descriptive evaluation. A UK summary of community action projects on poverty and health[3] has been followed up to obtain latest details. Descriptions of how schemes have been established and carried out give some valuable insight into how the processes of addressing poverty and health in young people can be approached. One of the most powerful tools of evaluation is the collecting of stories, that is inviting the young people to tell their experience as they see it rather than in a way which is confined to answers to a researcher's questions.[4] Usually, however, the evaluations appear to have been included either as an afterthought or with rather modest aims, and they do not give sufficient attention to exploring young people's views. This is probably because evaluation is seen as difficult and a poor relation to 'research'. Also there may be confusion about whose role it is to do the evaluation – the workers' or independent researchers'. The consequence is that opportunities are lost because sources of help to design and implement the evaluation are not sought. This may often be a fault of both the providers of the project and the sponsors, each assuming the other will take care of the evaluation.

It is also important to note that evaluation is not just at an individual project level. The wider context of information collection and baseline measurements are part of the effectiveness evaluation picture.

The key features of evaluation that need to be considered are:

- service outputs such as number of contacts made by young people and number of hours worked by professionals and volunteers;
- service processes in the form of operational and case study descriptions; and
- service outcomes also in case study form.

OUTCOMES

Most preventive work is not exclusively related to an outcome of behaviour change. Behaviour change over time can be a reductionist measurement, particularly in young people who are subject to change of circumstance, through transitions that usually include movement from a study area. Measurement of change in knowledge, attitude and skills development is also important.

RELIANCE ON THE VIEWS OF SERVICE WORKERS AND YOUNG PEOPLE

The net result of the above aspects of deficient information is that considerable reliance has to be put on the views of service providers which are frequently seen in print and heard in everyday practice. The views of young people themselves are less prominent in many of the published reports. It is apparent in what service providers, and young people themselves, say, that factors which may not be researched or evaluated can be the most important. For example, the empathy of staff towards young people is often mentioned as being crucial to successful interaction. Another factor is the amount of time that is available to be allocated to each young person in addressing one by one what are nearly always multiple problems. A further quality is expertise in solving a problem or knowing someone who can.

KEY MESSAGES

Controlled research must pay more attention to process description.

Evaluation guidelines are required for interventions in a variety of settings and circumstances.

Preventive work is not exclusively related to behaviour change and outcomes. Knowledge, attitude change and skills development, as well as use of services, are important measures.

The views of service staff and the young people they work with are important.

SERVICES FOR YOUNG PEOPLE: AREAS FOR IMPROVEMENT

HEALTH SERVICES NEED TO BE MORE PROACTIVE

Health services are often characterised by other statutory caring services, such as social services, as being strongly influenced by the 'medical model'. This model is one of tackling a defined pathological process, which in some cases can be inoculated against and in other cases can be treated with a drug or with a surgeon's knife. It is a model which anticipates clear solutions for circumscribed problems, and is increasingly a model recognised within medicine as inappropriate for treating the whole person of any age. However, it continues to influence the way doctors and nurses think and act and it may create a barrier, particularly for problems in the context of poverty, because there are no simple solutions and the health professional can easily be discouraged. Sometimes discouragement is manifested as 'victim blaming' and this may erect impenetrable barriers.

Providing general practice for young people in deprived populations requires dedication and organisation.

> **An example of general practice effort to reach deprived young people[5]**
>
> *Design*
>
> A team of general practitioners and nurses in Stockton-on-Tees gave special attention to young people living on a housing estate, described as 'severely deprived'. They made themselves more available both in the surgery and out in the community.
>
> *Results*
>
> Immunisations were completed for 72% of 5–15 year olds, compared with only 44% at the start of the programme, although immunisation rates for 5–15 year olds were still below those in a comparison population from a private housing area. The rate for having a smear test for cervical cancer in people aged 17–19 was raised from 57 to 67%. Less successful was an attempt to increase the percentage of 17–19 year olds who had a recorded method of contraception.

KEY MESSAGE

A well-organised service can improve uptake of preventive health measures but some young people will still miss out.

Immunisation boosters against diphtheria, tetanus, polio, measles and German measles for teenagers can be given by a general practice or by the school health services. Immunisation rates of 90 per cent plus are expected for these programmes. There is good evidence that a school health service which links up with well-organised practices, such as the one in Stockton-on-Tees, can ensure that deprived communities achieve a high uptake of immunisation so there should be no reason for young people in poverty to miss immunisation, providing they are accessing the services. Although many general practices are keen to give these immunisations, the school health services continue to be a valuable way of reaching young people who are still attending school and may find it easier to be immunised with colleagues at school rather than make a special appointment to see their general practitioner.[6]

GENERAL PRACTICE NEEDS TO LINK WITH OTHER RESOURCES FOR YOUNG PEOPLE

An east London general practitioner has described the experience of setting up a teenage clinic in two general practices, thereby approaching all 13–17 year olds in the practices directly.[7] They achieved only a 7 per cent attendance rate among all those invited.

The success rate was little better when 15 and 16 year olds were invited to a clinic for booster doses of tetanus and polio vaccine – just 12 per cent attended. It was concluded that general practitioners may need to be more proactive in routine consultations, allow flexibility in appointment systems, and above all, ensure confidentiality. They should also be prepared to work in schools and other non-traditional settings, working more closely with other agencies both within and outside the health sector. We have talked with a general practice in a Dorset market town, where health visitors have for three years run a clinic for 15 year olds. They managed to achieve a 57 per cent attendance from boys and 59 per cent from girls. They would now like to explore whether they are attracting those most in need: do attendances reflect the overall pattern of their young person population, and are young people from deprived communities attending in sufficient numbers? Also, the details of young person contacts with other members of the team need to be checked for the possibility of opportunistic 'screening'. In addition, it was felt that links with local schools could be improved, perhaps through initiatives such as an opportunity for pupils to receive some computer messaging about the teenage clinic. Since both the other practices in the town run teenage clinics there should not be a problem 'advertising' the service, since all the practices could participate.

KEY MESSAGE

Health services should be more proactive and link up with other services to form an attractive source of help for young people.

YOUNG PEOPLE AND THE PROVISION OF ADVISORY CENTRES/CLINICS

Research into health clinics for young people has identified that confidentiality is repeatedly referred to by young people as the most important factor when attending clinics or speaking to health professionals. This is closely followed by the 'attitudes' of staff and the need for a 'good listener'. A recent report investigating health service provision of young people's clinics stresses the importance of '... specially appointed reception staff' and a '... welcoming atmosphere'.[8] The respondents in a research project into young people's services in

Avon highlight this issue through reference to young people's feelings of awkwardness and embarrassment when ancillary clinic staff respond to them in a judgemental way or are inquisitive and fail to observe their need for privacy.[9] It was commented that '... when offered the chance to be interviewed with a friend many [interviewees] welcomed the opportunity with alacrity'.

A similar study in the north west found that young people attending a clinic in the Manchester area were often more comfortable in consultations with a peer present.[10] This appeared to have a positive effect on the number of under-16 males who attended the clinic. This age group is extremely difficult to reach, but in the Manchester study many of the new male attendees were introduced by friends. Young men are frequently marginalised in mainstream clinics which focus on young women and emphasis is put on family planning and the prevention of pregnancy. It is interesting to note here that a survey of 1,400 young people in Wales found that the three issues related to sexuality and sexual health which both young men and young women would like more information about are abortion, emergency contraception and issues surrounding homosexuality and lesbianism.[11]

The success of the Manchester clinic is also attributed to there being no lower age limit for clients. For example, 'curious' 11 year olds were not turned away, instead they were given a tour of the clinic and encouraged to ask questions. However, one of the clinics in the Avon study[10] was accused by Tory MP, Nicholas Winterton, of '... encouraging under-age sex' because young boys were seen cycling around in the vicinity of the clinic with inflated condoms on their heads and using them as waterbombs.[12] But it is suggested that it is this very openness which has contributed to lower conception rates in other European countries, along with higher rates of GNP per capita and more favourable income distribution.[13] Low birth rates among young teenage women, in the Netherlands for example, may reflect the non-moralistic attitudes of service providers, an accessible network of clinics and confidentiality.

The accessibility of clinics is of particular importance in rural areas where there is often less public transport and where fewer services are provided. Rural areas present their own particular problems: both confidentiality and anonymity are often difficult to maintain; there may be attitudes to young people's sexuality which is still frequently treated as a 'taboo' subject; after school hours clinics are difficult to access because so many young people are 'bussed' in to their schools; and poverty is often 'hidden' and not given the same priority as urban deprivation.[13] A recent report on young people's use of emergency contraception stated that '... areas of socio-economic deprivation should be targeted' to give more young people information about the provision of relevnt services. This is one of the areas where young people have asked for more information.[14]

Research does suggest that face-to-face contact and a continuum of service provision, which enhances the giving of information, can be beneficial to young people's sexual health[15] – the Avon research, for example, suggested that written information and leaflets are often difficult to assimilate. Research in Oxfordshire involved asking young people, in a wide range of secondary schools, their opinion of a selection of health promotion leaflets. It was found that there was a very clear selection of the preferred leaflets, with one or two regarded as brilliant and the remainder as rubbish.[6]

Some clinics need to develop special expertise for a particular situation, for example drug abuse in young mothers. Significant numbers of young female drug abusers under 20 are appearing in areas like Liverpool where a special effort has been made at the Liverpool Women's Hospital.[16]

Liverpool Women's Hospital initiative for drug abusing mothers (including young people)

A confidential non-judgemental approach.

Guidelines for care shared with drug agencies, social work and probation.

Outreach antenatal care to local drug dependency unit.

Regular social work review.

Methadone replacement therapy.

SUCCESSFUL CHARACTERISTICS OF CLINICS/CENTRES FOR YOUNG PEOPLE

Clinics and centres for young people exhibit certain characteristics when they are successful:[7-10, 14]

- There is obvious concern for confidentiality with private areas made available for 'clerking' and dispensing.
- Specially-trained reception staff are able to relate to young people.
- Opening hours fit around young people.

- Clinics are accessible to main transport routes.
- Young people have been consulted about ways of making the practice more user friendly through postcards, leaflets and magazines.
- The service is widely advertised.
- There are a large number of young people coming on a friend's recommendation.
- There is easy access to sources of advice on welfare benefits, jobs, training and housing.
- There is staff access to advice for problems requiring special expertise.
- There is continuity of service.
- The service is alert to warning signals such as suicide intent.

KEY MESSAGE

Essential service characteristics of advisory centres for young people are well-known and should be broadcast.

MENTAL HEALTH

You're trying to put your finger in the dike and hold the water back if you keep trying to increase patient contact in specialist mental health. And for young people in care there is a 40 per cent prevalence of severe emotional or psychiatric disturbance. It's 15 per cent in the general population, so it's a major issue for all adolescents. Their emotional well-being is a major issue because lots of them try to commit suicide.

Bolton Health Service Consultant in BYPASS, The Awareness of
Health Report 1995[17]

The NHS Health Advisory Reports on child and adolescent mental health services and on drug misuse in young people both stress the importance of the first 'tier' of service that must be attractive to young people and perceptive to their needs.[18,19] The proposed four tiers of service structure recommended in these two reports seem over-elaborate, particularly as they imply that the first tier of service may not involve 'the ability to practise in circumstances that are appropriate to young people'. This approach may perpetuate the divisions between primary and secondary healthcare within which it might be thought that only paediatricians understand children and only child and adolescent psychiatrists understand young people.

Appleby and colleagues reported a study which showed that in 61 suicide cases of under-35s there were increased consultations with the general practitioner shortly before the suicide and in only two cases had the general practitioner recorded concern about possible suicide risk.[20] There is no guarantee that early recognition of depression and suicidal intentions will be effective but it makes sense to reorient the services to make it more likely that underlying problems can be revealed.

'Help I need somebody'

Design

A Birmingham project consulted a wide range of young people and asked them to identify a current problem or concern and to nominate a person/agency who could help. Support was given when they approached their chosen person. The young people identified the barriers to asking for help and then kept a record of the help they had received.

Results

The expressed barriers were:

- not being taken seriously;
- services not for them;
- service providers won't speak 'my language';
- don't know where to go;
- might meet someone I know;
- parents will be told;
- don't want to be embarrassed.

Their recorded views led to the production by the young people of a 'Rough Guide', *Help, Advice and Information for Young People*.[21]

A Birmingham City-wide, free, confidential, young people focused, open-door counselling agency, which has existed for 29 years, is funded almost entirely through voluntary contributions and staffing. There are 30 counsellors running 90 counselling sessions per week. Current new referrals seen are around 15 per month; many young people require more than six weeks' counselling; the main presenting issues relate to physical and sexual abuse, often with presenting issues of self-harm, eating disorders, depression and substance abuse.[22]

> My doctor is stupid and I won't go. He's had me in tears because he just didn't want to know. And you don't just see one GP you see a different one every time you go. Anyway the receptionist gave me a lot of grief...just like the Social Services. If you can get away from Social Services then that's a good thing. Well it was for me anyway
>
> A frequent attender at the 'Bypass Centre' in Bolton.[17]

RESEARCH ON SOCIAL WORK INTERVENTIONS

A recent review of twenty research studies of child protection refers to the question 'would some children caught in the child protection net (Section 47 of the Children Act) benefit more from family support under Section 17 of the Children Act?'[23] Section 47 covers enquiries to establish whether the local authority needs to take action to safeguard a young person, whereas in Section 17 the emphasis is for local authorities to work with the family and young person in the family home and defines 'in need' as 'is unlikely to achieve or maintain, or to have the opportunity of achieving or maintaining, a reasonable standard of health or development without the provision of services by the local authority'. The review develops this by stating, 'after all, the circumstances of families dealt with under Sections 17 and 47 of the Act are frequently much the same, as are the services they ultimately receive'. However, if questions of abuse are in the air, the intervention is framed differently and parents are likely to be less receptive to social workers than if that approach were directed at helping a vulnerable child in need. The consequences of choosing one route or the other can be considerable. The researchers showed that resources were more likely to be allocated if the child were suspected of being abused. Placing his or her name on the register was often a way of getting help for a child, although the family members often disagreed with the procedure.

One of the studies reviewed looked at child protection practices in English local authorities.[24] Two messages emerged from the study:

- While the child protection system came to the rescue of some children in grave danger, large numbers were being drawn in whose needs tended to be neglected as soon as it was established that protective intervention as such was not required.
- The evidence concerning case outcome showed that the specialist resources that might make a difference to the development of protected children were largely controlled by the education and health authorities.

Another recent review by the Department of Health, which incorporates three specially-funded studies, provides some valuable insight into the factors which influence young people who are assessed as in need of care.[25] In one of the three studies social workers spent a lot of time discussing drug misuse and it was reported that attempts by professionals to encourage change, by acting as a mentor, were effective only if done within a relationship of trust. Trust between social workers or carers and young people takes time to develop and for many young people 'looked after', continuity of relationships was in short supply. Nonetheless, in half of the cases where social workers tried to change young people's habits the intervention was considered to have been successful.

Sex education was frequently inadequate for young people living away from home. This may have been the result of frequent placement changes and school absenteeism. Success in tackling sexual issues was found to depend on the quality of the relationship between the young person and the social worker or carer, and the willingness of the professional to broach the matter. One study found that within 24 months of leaving care one-third of young people had become parents. The study's finding that over half of pregnancies were unplanned suggests social workers' anxieties about scant counselling in sexual matters appeared well-founded.

The research showed that supportive work with African and Asian Muslim communities was not common. Some of these families were unaware of what services were available, others were unwilling to expose private family matters to public scrutiny, while some were fearful of official reactions. A combination of these factors may be germane to the reluctance of African and Asian parents to seek social services' help. Indeed, most referrals involving teenagers from these communities emanated from other agencies or from the young people themselves. Problems of working with families of different religious, cultural or ethnic backgrounds were compounded when social workers had little experience of the communities or their belief systems.

KEY MESSAGES

There should be continuing input by the same social worker acting as a mentor.

Social workers must be persistent in creating support for young people, while acting as their champion.

Social workers must be able to engage actively with the young person.

VOLUNTARY ORGANISATIONS

Voluntary organisations can provide alternative forms of social support which promote health through actions to divert young people from care or other legal proceedings, through practical help for disabled young people and help for young people leaving care. The NCH Action for Children Rural Youth Project has run six rural youth action programmes and one in Perth and Kinross. Several key factors have been reported.

Perth and Kinross Rural Youth Project[12]

Design

- aims to divert young people aged 12-16 from the formal care and legal systems unless care and protection issues deem otherwise;
- complements statutory and other voluntary organisations;
- involves volunteers from the local community;
- features group and individual work, including involvement of parents to help young people develop social skills.

Results

- 64% showed positive improvement and there was special success in preventing repeat criminal offences;
- young people perceive the involvement as less threatening and more confidential than statutory social work.

Barnardo's has examples of successful support for disabled young people and for young people recently in local authority care.

Grove Road Project

Design

Supports disabled young people and their families by providing:

- a lodgings scheme which aims to offer accommodation across a range of lodgings with accredited lodgings providers which meets the needs of disabled young people. These are ordinary householders who are approved to take lodgers after a home study and panel approval;
- a counselling service which aims to offer a service which is accessible to young people either directly or via other services. Priority is given to young people unable to use other services due to limited access and restricted choice.

Barnardo's, 1996.[26]

> **The Aberdeenshire 16+ project**
>
> **Design**
>
> Aims to work in partnership with Aberdeenshire Rural Council to develop a comprehensive, community-based service with young people who request support during the transition period from being looked after by the local authority. The type of support offered includes preparation for leaving care on either an individual or a group basis; support in moving on from residential care, foster care, board and lodgings etc; and support in Barnado's bedsits.
>
> Barnardo's, 1996.[26]

These examples illustrate the need to consider various ways of providing 'social work' for young people and the common need, with education and health services, to explore variations such as the use of 'peer' volunteers. A review of 10 voluntary service projects for children and young people identified three models of service which were: a client focused model run by professional staff with little neighbourhood outreach, rather like the statutory services; a neighbourhood model with open–door local participation and neighbourhood identification; and a community development model similar to the neighbourhood model but with local control.[27] The neighbourhood models were favoured as having more potential for success, since they were able to engage local resources in ways which enabled greater insight into problems and a greater range of options for support.

KEY MESSAGES

Young people may be more comfortable with voluntary workers who are involved as part of the local community.

Practical help is required by young people in a variety of situations.

HEALTH EDUCATION IN SCHOOLS WILL NOT CHANGE BEHAVIOUR OF MANY SCHOOL LEAVERS

For two decades, health education about smoking has been embodied in classroom practice, yet seen through the eyes of adolescents, especially adolescents at loggerheads with authority, what the school stands for in terms of adult and establishment values, didactic teaching, and possibly boredom, irrelevance and alienation, may militate strongly against the possible success of health education within its confines. Since they can express that disenchantment by doing what they are told not to do, they have a motive to smoke. The wisdom on smoking, together with other rejected adult values and attitudes, can be easily dumped at the school gates, leaving children to go free to get on with what is important, relevant and valued in their own lives. We must acknowledge this, and renew our efforts to find ways of reaching children on their own territory and on their own terms.[28]

This quotation echoes the views of North American commentators that those young people who are living in poverty and most likely to engage in health damaging behaviour are part of a 'school–oppositional culture'.[29] Young people within this culture will have tended to move through progressive stages of 'problem behaviour'. The first stage is the result of poor parenting, leading to low emotional attachment to parents, resistance to parental authority, early behavioural and emotional problems and generalised developmental immaturity with poor attention span and poor impulse control.

In the second stage at school, peers and teachers respond antagonistically to poorly socialised behaviour and the child develops an alienation to school which manifests in the teenage years as lack of interest or enthusiasm for all school activities and rebellion, with rejection of conventional social norms about drug use, and safe sex. In many case the young person is simply not in school for any significant time, but on the streets.

Health education, whether it is a basic knowledge programme, covered by the core curriculum, or enhanced modules with efforts to build self-esteem, acquire social skills and the ability to say no to health damaging temptations, has largely failed in attempts to change and maintain changes to healthier behaviour. What is striking is that in most cases the special efforts have not been targeted at high risk young people but usually at a whole school population, within which high risk individuals do not participate, as we see in the following sections.

SEX EDUCATION

An overview of research into sex education identified only 12 out of 73 studies which were methodologically sound.[30] Of these only one, which was a North American study of sex education for homeless young people, reported effective change of behaviour.[31] This was a non-randomised but controlled study of sex education, delivered by male and female trained leaders to groups of approximately 10 runaway 11–18 year olds, who were predominantly Black or Hispanic: 64 per cent were girls. The intervention addressed general knowledge about AIDS, coping skills, access to healthcare and other resources and individual barriers to safer sex. Outcomes which showed improvement as a result of the intervention were increased condom use and decreased reports of high risk sexual behaviour. However the follow-up time was only for six months.

In the UK, a report considered the investment of medical time in association with a life skills approach to sex education in comprehensive secondary schools and studied this over a three-year period of programme build up.[32] They were able to show an improvement in knowledge as a result of 30 hours of sex education but their claims that behavioural change follows were not strongly substantiated. A North American report suggests that age of onset of sexual intercourse in a deprived population could be delayed by a peer led intervention.[33]

Peer led education to delay sexual activity

Design

In low income neighbourhoods a randomised controlled study of a programme led by trained and supervised peer leaders, one boy and one girl for each group, who presented 10-session programmes in 19 different schools.

Results

Telephone follow up, one year after the programme was presented, showed that in schools receiving the programme only 24% had begun having sex compared with 39% in comparison schools, where the programme was not given.

This underlines the need to question the concentration of resources currently being devoted to sex education for all schoolchildren when it might be more appropriate to target efforts towards those most in need of information and, perhaps more important, to ensure that the messages are clear and attractive. For example, there may need to be as much concentration on use of the morning-after pill as on avoiding unprotected sex for young people who may regard unprotected sex as 'brilliant as a smoke' or a 'fix' in their particular situation. Extra resources for sex education tend to be provided by health promotion departments, and usually consist of elaborate support for the development of peer education programmes, most commonly targeted at whole classrooms and for the reasons given above these are not likely to be taken up by the high risk groups.

If a school has the resources it may be able to ensure special support for teenagers in poverty who become pregnant.

A school for pregnant teenagers[34]

Design
Controlled study of a school in the USA which provides education, social and medical support to low income teenage girls through workers of mixed ethnic background. Some of the issues handled included arranging day care for the baby, remaining in school to complete at least a high school degree, delaying subsequent childbearing, coping with family conflict, and finding housing.

Results
Mothers who dropped out before seven weeks – 75% became pregnant again within five years.

Mothers who stayed beyond seven weeks – 50% became pregnant again within five years.

In the UK pregnant teenagers are provided for within the mainstream school system but often there will not be extra time or resources to give to the complex problems the girls face. The Rowan Project in Rotherham is a Barnardo's project, in partnership with the local education authority, which provides for flexible teaching to allow young mothers to care for their babies at school and provides out of school support and appropriate childcare facilities.[26]

KEY MESSAGES

Sex education may delay age of intercourse but it needs social support services and access to emergency contraception to sustain its effects.

Resources should be targeted at those most at risk.

Special support is required to maintain education for young mothers.

HEALTH EDUCATION ON DRUG USE

Drug education in schools has been mainly targeted at whole school populations to stop them using drugs. A randomised controlled study of a smoking education programme, taught under normal classroom conditions to 11–12 year olds, was run in Welsh and English schools.[35] Lessons focused on peer, family and media influences on smoking, with emphasis on practising skills for managing social situations in which smoking occurs. No consistent significant differences in smoking behaviour, health knowledge, beliefs or values were found between the teacher/peer led group and the control group. The authors concluded that more comprehensive intervention than school health education alone will be needed to reduce teenage smoking.

Although this and other anti-smoking programmes in schools have failed it was thought that programmes covering alcohol and cannabis as well as smoking might succeed. There have been no UK published studies of such an approach but one study in the USA randomly assigned schools to an 11-lesson programme on smoking, alcohol and cannabis, which was adult or peer led.[36] The study was run in 30 schools for 11–12 year olds, many of which had a 50 per cent or more minority ethnic population. By age 16 no significant effects of the programme on drug taking could be detected.

It has been suggested that programmes should continue longer in the form of booster sessions. This was tested in a programme in the USA. Teacher led sessions were followed by a booster after one and two years.[37] The results indicated that more substantially resourced teacher led programmes, with booster sessions, failed to reach the disaffected young person who drops out of education by 16 or earlier. This is the group that is most likely to be at risk of drug misuse.

An intensive programme for 'high risk youth' in the USA has been reported. The analysis of this programme showed some stemming of drug control problems.[38]

An intervention for high risk drug users

Design

Students aged 14–17 in four high schools, who were at high risk of school dropout and drug abuse, were randomly selected. They were allocated either to receive for five months sessions of group problem solving of each participant's issues and skills training geared to real life problems raised by the participants or to receive usual teaching. 30% allocated to the intervention group and 16% allocated to the control group refused to participate. Process evaluations included monitoring by a classroom observer of exposure to specific skills training and examples of teacher and peer support.

Results

21% of the intervention group and 19% of the control dropped out of the study. Non-completers were likely to be older and more involved in drugs.

The intervention group showed a tendency to curb their progression from legal to illegal drugs and showed a significant decrease in drug control problems, together with improvements in actual and perceived school performance, and an increase in peer and school bonding.

Some of the practical problems of recruitment and programme participation in the above study might have been avoided if this intervention were featured not just within the school, but also included other involvements with the local community.

KEY MESSAGE

There should be less emphasis on classroom drug use education in schools and more attention to supporting those with a drug problem to combat it, drawing on resources inside and outside the school.

INVOLVEMENT OF YOUNG PEOPLE

ETHICS OF INTERVENING

Before contemplating an intervention to help young people change their behaviour it is necessary to predict whether more harm than good will result from intervening. It is essential to listen to the views of young people, to respect their autonomy and to involve them in decisions regarding action aimed towards a change of behaviour.

ETHICAL PRINCIPLES UNDERLYING INTERVENTIONS TO HELP YOUNG PEOPLE CHANGE BEHAVIOUR

There are several underlying ethical principles that should be taken into consideration:

- must cause more good than harm;
- must listen to their views;
- must respect the young person's autonomy;
- must involve them in decisions for action;
- must provide support during the changes.

There have been many contributions to developing theories of health behaviour change during the last fifty years and the main influences on young people are summarised in the following section.

A HEALTH BEHAVIOUR MODEL FOR YOUNG PEOPLE

A health behaviour model should include the following:[39-43]

- influence of family and friends and opinion leaders;
- knowledge with views on seriousness of the disease, personal susceptibility and whether health behaviour protects;
- values, attitudes and motivation to change;
- self-esteem and efficacy;
- social skills;
- intention to change; and
- perseverance in change.

Bunton and colleagues expressed the view that, although there has been increasing recognition of the role of social and cultural variables in explaining the adoption of new behaviours, there is still too great an emphasis on the use of psychologically orientated models.[44] This would seem to be reflected in strategies such as *Health of the Nation* which can be interpreted as giving a predominant influence to the view that the responsibility for healthy change rests firmly with the individual.[45] This is in marked contrast to the assessment of influences on the health of poor young people that was considered in Chapter 2.

Poor young people are less likely to acquire knowledge about health damaging behaviour. They are more likely to be influenced by their immediate circle of family and friends, and to be in a culture with attitudes and behaviours which are geared more to seeking comfort than being healthy. They may also have low self-esteem, self-efficacy and poorly developed social skills. Their perspectives on the need to change to more healthy behaviour may be very different to that of those who are attempting to help them change their 'unhealthy behaviour'. Research on the lifestyles of mothers on low income, many of whom were young, showed that young women who cared for others and had few material resources to do so, developed coping strategies using cigarettes.[46]

KEY MESSAGE

The sociocultural factors which influence young people's health behaviour must be explored before possible interventions are considered.

A range of examples of the involvement of young people in health promoting projects follows:

Lifeline action for young drug users in Manchester[47]

Design

Lifeline is a non-statutory drug agency that has developed the involvement of young women in the design of cartoon leaflets on drugs misuse. The girls advised on language, dress, attitudes, issues of importance and changed details time and time again, to ensure that they were culturally spot-on. Time and time again they stressed the importance of creating characters who would be 'cool' – funny, a bit stupid, but a perfect medium for communicating key messages regarding issues such as weight loss and keeping up with the lads when taking drugs.

Results

They felt it important that there weren't too many different health messages conveyed in the cartoons, as people would think them too 'preachy', so the cartoons were combined with pages of text, reinforcing the key messages, such as what constitutes a healthy diet and how to avoid dehydration. 'Even the boys enjoy reading about the antics of Clare and Josie!' Over 50,000 leaflets in the Clare and Josie range have been sold.

DAFFY – Drama and fun and food workshops for young carers[48]

Design

A new initiative to run special days when young carers can meet together for some impromptu drama, art and craft. The content is constructed by young carers to have fun and in so doing explore some of the frustrations and joys of helping to care and feel responsible for someone. Practical back-up is provided in the form of extra help at home and transport to the workshops.

When I came to BYPASS I was a real mess. I didn't have any
confidence especially being on the street. I had counselling in hospital
and it never worked for me. But here the counsellor asks me how I
feel about things. In hospital they said I had schizophrenia. It scares
me if this place wasn't open and I had to go somewhere like that.[17]

BYPASS centre[16]

Design

This young people's advice and support centre is run by and for young people in
Bolton. They receive multi-agency service support and their services include:

- sexual health peer education project;
- drug support project;
- services for young people in care;
- dietary advice service;
- mental health counselling.

Results

The distinguishing features of this service are:

- it is a centre young people regard as their own;
- it manages to achieve complex tasks with few resources;
- it has a pleasant and welcoming atmosphere which young people find attractive;
- it has a mixture of staff who are both interesting and interested;
- it has a range of professionals who share the commitment and enthusiasm of
  the centre; and
- it is often difficult to tell staff from volunteers/participants.

KEY MESSAGE

**Young people, if involved, come up with different ideas
from adults and these are likely to be more successful.**

INTERVENTIONS TO SUPPORT YOUNG PEOPLE AS PARENTS

Health visitors and volunteers working with young parents have had
notable success in giving young people confidence to cope with
parenting. Olds *et al.* showed the beneficial effect of nurse home
visiting for two years after the birth of a child to poor teenagers,
particularly in planning repeat pregnancies and returning to education
or finding employment.[49] It was noticed in this study that those most
likely to benefit had better baseline support, for example from a

boyfriend. Another example of support for young parents is the 45 Cope Street project.[50]

---

45 Cope Street[49]

45 Cope Street is a preventive health project working with young mothers aged 16–25 and their children in inner-city Nottingham.

Design

A team of health visitors, nursery nurses and midwives identified the needs of young deprived parents, working with groups in structured and unstructured ways and through practical-based activities. Creche support was provided. An informal process of exploring mothers' thoughts and feelings was formalised by anonymous participant recording over 15 months.

Results

It was concluded that the centre had helped some women to achieve more emotional stability and self-confidence. Depression, lack of money and support and the need for a break featured strongly, as did the need for information on job opportunities.

The value of the group in providing mothers with a break from their babies and young children was also apparent. Developments of the scheme included a parent support network and a drop-in morning for pregnant mothers.

Community nursing services felt that the provision had offered new opportunities for clinical staff to work in a different environment and thereby acquire new skills.

One problem noted in earlier studies of parent support programmes was the non-involvement of fathers in the programme, which may have significant implications, especially because of the fragile nature of the relationship between teenage mothers and teenage fathers.[51] The mothers' participation in the programme has in most cases contributed to significant personal growth, and not only have some of the fathers resented this, but often they have been developing in directions different from those of their partner.

Sometimes health service resources are insufficient for a concentration of service on those most in need and voluntary project workers may be recruited. Such voluntary recruits may be from the same background as the young parents in need and this may enhance communication. A randomised controlled study in Dublin looked at the deployment of volunteer, non-professional 'Community Mothers', who were recruited from the same deprived community, each to provide home visiting support, in addition to routine public health nurse support, with up to 15 visits.[52]

Peer volunteers supporting young parents[52]

Design
Randomised controlled study of a child development support programme developed, for use by health visitors but the shortage of health visitors in Dublin led to the alliance with volunteers, who were specially trained. Each volunteer undertook home visits, frequently 10 or more.

Results
The 'Community Mothers' were able to increase the young parents' self-esteem as judged by reported reduction of tiredness, headaches, feeling miserable and staying in. Their ability to cope with a young baby was enhanced and this was reflected in improved immunisation rates, fewer accidents and a better diet for the babies and the mothers.

KEY MESSAGE

Young parents benefit from targeted support which is built up with their involvement and can be enhanced by young person peer involvement.

STRENGTHEN COMMUNITY ACTION

Action by one organisation will have a limited impact on the health of young people. Whole community interventions are more difficult to evaluate but may have considerable potential.

Accident prevention for young people in an inner city[53]

Design
A controlled study of a 'Safe Kids – Healthy Neighbourhood' coalition in Harlem, New York, which worked to renovate playgrounds, involved young people in safe, supervised activities that would teach them useful skills such as dance, art, sports, horticulture and carpentry; provided injury and violence prevention education; provided cycle helmets at reasonable cost, and initiated a pedestrian safety programme.

Results
Accidents in 5-16 year olds declined over a three-year period and although it was not possible to be sure that this was a direct result of local actions, there were certainly some promising features of young people's involvement which could be tried in the UK.

A community initiative to prevent drugs misuse[54]

Design

A controlled drug education programme in eight communities in Kansas City, USA, which included: 10 sessions of drugs use resistance skills training in schools, for 12 and 13 year olds; a parent organisation programme for reviewing school prevention policy, and training parents in positive parent-child communication skills; a training of community leaders in the organisation of a drug abuse prevention task force and mass media coverage.

Results

The total programme appeared to have some beneficial effect in reducing use of nicotine and marijuana, but not alcohol, in both 'high risk' and 'low risk' young people. The methodology of this study was flawed in the sampling and selection processes, which were neither random, nor clearly described, but study of this kind of multi-component approach might be considered in the UK.

Healthy eating support for young people[55]

Design

A descriptive evaluation of the Barri Grubb Food Project in a low income area of Edinburgh which developed a mobile healthy, low cost and small portion food shop. It was driven around the area and parked at local churches, cafes and schools and served up to 350 customers, particularly children, each weekday.

Results

Good uptake in primary schools. Developments for a continued project include increased advertising, more liaison with community groups to increase the range of foods and to sell non-food household necessities. Also more contact with non-participating schools, particularly secondary schools, and an increase in health education by staff is also envisaged. The project has, however, been dogged by uncertainty of funding.

A young persons' drop-in centre[56]

Design

A worker employed by the health service set up a local steering group in Blandford, Dorset, to identify local health problems, one of which was boredom in young people. Interviews with young people were followed by their involvement in planning and running a drop-in centre open several days each week. It also received funding from the town council, district council, youth service and a charitable trust.

Results

In 1995, 7,029 visits were made to the centre by young people, most of whom were aged 15-20. 433 visits were either for sex education or advice on drugs. The other visits were for advice on welfare benefits, training and employment, transport and housing. The project has had some uncertainties about continued funding.

An important issue which is frequently mentioned by those engaged in community projects is that it is necessary to have the support of statutory services, particularly to ensure continuity of the project. It is apparent that local people feel very angry if this support is not forthcoming and as they see it 'the plug is pulled' on their initiatives. Statutory services may also have an important role in helping to stabilise the running of projects.

KEY MESSAGE

Community action, supported by statutory services, and based on young people identifying the important issues, can harness many sources of resources to run an appropriate service.

THE PATHWAYS TO A YOUNG PEOPLE'S SERVICE

In this chapter we have explored initiatives and interventions to improve the health of young people in poverty. Isolated action within one statutory setting, or by one statutory service, is unlikely to be successful and may be wasting resources which could be better invested in a multi-agency approach.

It is apparent that many initiatives for the health of young people either ignore poverty, such as those that target all school children, or they struggle to provide sufficient time and expertise to address the problems, such as general practices trying to provide an attractive service for all young people, and social workers having to allocate their already over-committed time to health maintenance work.

The way forward lies in starting at the consumer end rather than the service provider end of the spectrum. What do young people in poverty want to do about their health and who do they want to help them? Instead of perpetuating the present approach of each service struggling on its own to help young people, there should be an integrated approach, as exemplified by the young people's advisory service centres with outreach services. Such services are attractive to funders, including local district, borough and town councils, community councils, local grant-making trusts, national grant-making trusts, the National Lottery Charities Board, the Lottery Sports

Fund, the Arts Council Lottery Fund and the Millennium Commission.

The statutory services supporting this approach should also appraise their own investments for young people's health. Most of the health authorities invest in health promotion services that are still dominated by the idea that you can change schoolchild behaviour through health education. Those resources should be diverted to underpin young person advisory services, for example with outreach support. Some of the investment in health visiting services should be targeted to provide special support for vulnerable young parents rather than unnecessary child development testing for advantaged children. Social services should create a health maintenance arm for young people, and should combine their efforts with the broader activities of the voluntary sector.

Action is required at local, regional and national level to ensure that efforts are not dissipated. One of the commonest statements from fieldworkers in the health services for young people is that efforts on the ground are undermined by goverment inaction in curbing unhealthy advertising, and by the media not sending out the right messages about health problems in young people. In the following section there are some examples of what needs to be done at local, regional and national level.

LOCAL ACTION FOR YOUNG PEOPLE

In 1990 a development worker met and talked with 265 young men and women aged between 14 and 25 in 30 groups in the Durham and Chester le Street areas.[57] They recognised the need for a general support service, with staff trained in the special needs of young people, clear and explicitly defined boundaries of confidentiality and flexible opening hours. This was then discussed at a series of public meetings. Out of these meetings was born the concept of a centre specifically for young people which would be a central resource. It would operate on an informal basis but would have the potential to respond to specialist issues, problems or concerns young people might bring, and it would involve young people directly in its management.

Four schools helped with design and distribution of a 'problem checklist' completed by 126 respondents, 34 per cent of whom said that they would use a young people's centre. A further public meeting was held in late 1991 which considered this response and then set up a steering group of 25, half of whom were young people. Training for the steering group was provided by Save the Children, enabling a number of task groups to cover aspects such as running costs of the proposed centre, the writing of a constitution for the centre, and the planning and running of the meetings of the group, with an elected executive committee. The Durham Young People's Centre Association became a registered charity in late 1992.

Funding of £26,000 followed from the Health Authority, and efforts were made to secure a matching sum from other sources. The local MP opened a lobbying meeting in late 1993, at which young people put their case for the centre and local councillors, approached prior to the meeting, added their support. Five weeks later a joint finance grant of £26,000 was made to the centre and a new group of supporters came forward and became the advisory group. In 1994 a co-ordinator was appointed, Children in Need allocated £55,000 over a three-year period and premises were found for the centre. The practical arrangements for the centre included geographical accessibility, space for two clinical rooms, two secure offices and one information and storage area. Staff included a project co-ordinator, project worker, half-time secretarial support and a caretaker/cleaner.

A long but successful story of the efforts to launch the new service for young people show the essential elements to be:

- vision and flexibility;
- the continuing involvement of young people;
- organisation to achieve the tasks;
- commitment from key individuals; and
- networking.

The 1995/1996 annual report for the 'End House' Durham Young People's Centre records an ever-increasing number of young people coming to the centre, between 70 and 80 each month in early 1996.

End House Durham Young People's Centre

End House provides a one-stop shop where young people can meet socially but also access a range of services under one roof:

- open access sessions for information, support and counselling on three afternoons/early evenings per week, with additional counselling sessions throughout the week;
- leaflets, magazines and reports on young people's issues;
- coffee shop;
- laundry and shower facilities;
- sexual health and contraceptive clinic with open access, early evenings twice a week;
- computer terminal access to training opportunities;
- weekly young gay and bi-sexual group;
- meeting group for young people who have been in care;
- a support group for young people who have epilepsy;
- End House young people's group looking at producing a newsletter and video about the centre;
- access to housing and emergency accommodation advice;
- youth services HQ;
- the promotion of positive health on a holistic basis;
- the development of voluntary service.

The majority of young people using End House tend to fall within the ages of 14–18. Most of the contacts are in person rather than by phone and 88 per cent come on their own initiative. About one-third come because they have heard about the centre from a friend. The main issues and concerns young people come to End House with are health and sexuality, family arguments, breakdowns, bereavements, conflicts and violence, aspects of independent living and mental health.

REGIONAL ACTION FOR YOUNG PEOPLE

In 1995 the West Midlands Regional Health Authority allocated £20m for the enhancement of primary healthcare at community level and £1.25m was allocated to projects involving young people.[58] The fund is managed by a partnership of district health authorities, the city council, the family health services authority, and four community health councils. This primary care development group has been supported by a project team based at the Family Health Services Authority, with fieldwork undertaken by 12 constituency action teams (CATS), whose part-time membership has included general practitioners and local representatives from health, local authority and community health councils. A member of the project team had specific responsibility for projects involving young people.

MORI'S health research unit was commissioned to assess and recommend an evaluation strategy and a case study design was proposed, drawing mainly on qualitative techniques.

CAT young people's projects in Birmingham

Two-year, young people's forum led project in two constituencies for up to 16,000 11–18 year olds that will include mobile information service, training of youth and teaching staff, and training of young people as peer educators. £180,000 covers two full-time youth workers, a full-time health worker, a part-time clerical worker and sessional support staff.

Production of a young people's designed 'Rough Guide' to health and health-related services in Birmingham targeted at 14–19 year olds. Funding of £156,000 over three years will allow production of 20,000 guides.

New sexual health clinics and outreach service for 11–24 year olds, one clinic in each of two constituencies, with funding of £343,000 over three years to cover premises costs, a full-time outreach worker and a part-time development co-ordinator.

Youth club-based service to empower young teenagers. Funding of £38,000 over three years to provide part-time youth and health service workers.

School nutrition action group to improve school meals in 75 primary and secondary schools in Birmingham. Action involves young people's fora for developing school food policies. Funding of £176,000 over three years.

Individual needs assessment and curriculum consultancy and development to help five schools develop an appropriate sexual health curriculum. Funding of £20,000 over two years, plus £40,000 from the education department, will enable staff training and development.

Provision of an information centre and detached youth work mainly for 14–19 year olds on three housing estates. The focus will be on sexual health within a holistic health approach. Funding of £237,000 over three years covers cost of shop premises, two detached youth workers and two part-time information and counselling workers.

Underpinning an existing open-door counselling service for 14–24 year olds throughout the city. Funding of £67,000 over three years covers salary and training for the development and link liaison worker.

Mobile youth work bus in one ward. Funding of £100,000 for two years covers a full-time youth worker, two part-time workers, secretarial and clerical costs, plus running costs of the bus.

Other projects to be developed included a support service for young Asian people who are in conflict with their parents or communities and the provision of a drop-in cafe, advice and health information centre

---

KEY MESSAGES

A major commitment must be made to funding health services for young people.

Projects aimed specifically at improving the health of poor young people should be initiated.

There should be a serious effort to incorporate evaluation.

Interagency and cross professional working are essential.

NATIONAL ACTION: ADVOCACY

Doctors in Australia mounted a campaign in which they went out, usually at night, to deface billboards advertising tobacco products. Billboards Utilising Graffiti Against Unhealthy Products (BUGA UP) influenced politicians and schoolchildren in publicising the dangers of tobacco and their activities resulted in a phasing out of cinema and billboard advertising of cigarettes, an increase in tobacco tax, higher penalties for underage sales of tobacco and the phasing out of product sponsorship of sports functions. While the definite attribution of changes to BUGA UP activities is difficult, an impact on schoolchild smoking in the late 1980s may well have occurred (see Figure 3.1).

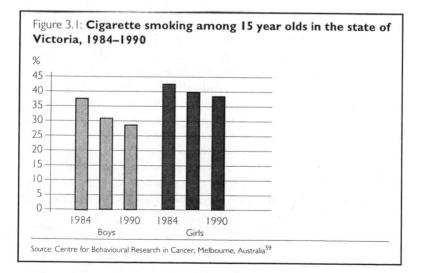

Figure 3.1: **Cigarette smoking among 15 year olds in the state of Victoria, 1984–1990**

Source: Centre for Behavioural Research in Cancer, Melbourne, Australia[59]

> ### KEY MESSAGE
>
> **If young people, doctors and politicians are united they can achieve major change.**

The part played by doctors in the previous example leads to the question whether there is scope for people working with young people to create similar spectacles regarding the circumstances of young people in poverty. An advocacy role has been bread and butter to voluntary organisations, but messages would be amplified if staff in the statutory services were to contribute more than just occasional letters to newspapers. Individual staff may be under-standably nervous about sticking their necks out but it should certainly not be difficult for professional associations to make a combined and concerted effort to publicise inequalities and preventable causes of ill health in young people.

NATIONAL ACTION ON TAXING AN UNHEALTHY PRODUCT

There are options for government to impose high taxes on products which harm young people's health, such as junk food, alcohol and tobacco. Tobacco products have a price elasticity in western nations of approximately -0.5, meaning that a 10 per cent rise in price causes a 5 per cent fall in demand.[60] Smoking cessation or reduction in low income groups is much more responsive to price rises than in higher income groups. For young men, income seems to be more influential than price.[61] For teenage women, however, price rises are likely to have a greater effect, although the effects of price and income would appear to be interrelated. Price rises for tobacco may cause problems for young people, but some think the long-term health benefits outweigh these. Others feel that, 'together the increased concentration of smoking among the poor and increases in income inequalities have ensured that tobacco tax has become the most regressive tax we have – the only effect such price rises have is to increase the hardship experienced by poor smokers, for them and for their children.'[62]

> **KEY MESSAGE**
>
> **Increasing the relative price of cigarettes will reduce smoking in young people but will cause some hardship to those with scarce funds.**

NATIONAL ADVERTISING AND PROMOTION

In the UK the national budget for health education rose from £8m to £45m between 1979 and 1996. Much of this is spent on health promotion through the media but a recent review could not identify one successful campaign for young people.[63] This review concluded that, 'even when all of the pre-conditions for success are present, changes in behaviour are usually small scale'. Another review discussed a government mass media campaign, costing £2m, aimed at heroin misuse in young people aged 13–20.[43] The apparent success of the campaign in raising awareness and affecting attitudes to recognise the dangers of heroin addiction were called into question by apparent important differences in the characteristics of the study and control populations. It was argued that even if the effects were real, there would have been more benefit in investing the money in local drug prevention services.

By contrast, the impact of advertising unhealthy products specifically aimed at young people seems to be widespread. Governments are beginning to recognise that tobacco advertising is of crucial importance in influencing children to start smoking. The power of media advertising has been illustrated in a negative sense by the impact of the Embassy Regal 'Reg' campaign to promote a brand of cigarettes. The use of a character that young people identified with caused government action for the campaign to be halted but it seems that its short appearance was sufficient to have a lasting impression on young smokers. As reported from Dundee, 11–15 year olds appear to have been influenced by the 'Reg' campaign to consider Embassy Regal the 'in' brand to smoke.[64]

Generally, however, cigarette advertising influences overall – rather than specific – attitudes to smoking. A questionnaire survey of 1,450 pupils in England aged 11–12 (the age range that coincides with the highest onset of smoking) concluded that '... cigarette advertising appears to increase children's awareness of smoking at a generic level and encourages them to take up the behaviour, beginning with any cigarettes which are available and affordable'.[65]

STOP SPONSORSHIP OF UNHEALTHY PRODUCTS

The sponsorship by tobacco companies of sporting events has a profound effect on young people's smoking habits. It has been argued that '... the most outrageous and deplorable example of circumvention of the voluntary agreement [between the manufacturers and the Department of Health] on cigarette advertising is the existence of massive cigarette brand promotions by means of sports sponsorship'.[66] In a survey Benson & Hedges was most frequently mentioned by young male smokers.[65] This is likely to be closely related to sports sponsorship because Benson & Hedges sponsors both cricket and snooker, shown regularly on television. The Australian example of replacing tobacco sponsorship of sporting events with health promotion sponsorship is a model that should be adopted in the UK.

KEY MESSAGES

Advertising and sponsorship of tobacco products are powerful negative influences on young people's health which could be reversed at a stroke.

A national health promotion budget for sports sponsorship should be created.

ACTION TO CURB UNHEALTHY PRODUCT SALES TO MINORS

The current legislation covering the sale of tobacco products in the UK is contained in the Children and Young Persons (Protection from Tobacco) Act 1991 and this shifted the onus of responsibility onto the retailer to ensure that the young person buying cigarettes is 16 or over. It was also made illegal to sell loose cigarettes in quantities under 10.[67] Large notices must be displayed stating that cigarettes and other tobacco products are sold only to people over 16, wherever these goods are sold, either over the counter or through vending machines. If a cigarette vending machine is used by a young person under 16 it can be removed and a penalty of £2,500 can be imposed on the owner of the machine or the person on whose premises it is kept.

This Act was the direct result of public health lobbying and was therefore expected to be an important advance in reducing smoking in young people. However, as in the USA, it has proved to be a difficult law to enforce. In Scotland there is particular concern at the possibility of children appearing as prosecution witnesses in court and they have ruled out the use of young volunteers for the purpose of gathering evidence. A recent review in the USA concluded that publicity about prosecutions may inadvertently raise the profile of the ease with which young people can obtain cigarettes, and may make the activity even more attractive.[68]

KEY MESSAGE

In spite of legal support it is difficult to cut off supply of cigarettes or other unhealthy products to the under–16s.

HOW THE MEDIA CAN HELP

A local health promotion service in Dorset has drawn up guidelines for suicide prevention with particular reference to young men, and this contains a section on how the media can help.[69] The guidelines state that:

> The media is seen as having two important roles to play in reducing the toll of young male suicides: informing the public about the causes of suicide and exploring the social and economic problems young men face; the development of practical guidelines on the reporting of suicide which, if implemented, can limit the risk of copycat suicides amongst young people.

Examples of how the the media can help in the prevention of suicide in young people include:

- avoiding simplistic explanations for suicide;
- debunking common myths about suicide;
- highlighting the underlying causes of suicide;
- including information on further sources of information and help;
- avoiding 'how to' descriptions of suicide in reports;
- avoiding repetitive ongoing coverage of suicide stories, especially of youth suicides; and
- not romanticising or glorifying suicide.

Many of these principles are also applicable to the other aspects of young people's health, covered in this chapter and they should receive wider attention and national as well as local action.

NATIONAL CO-ORDINATION OF ACTION

A report produced by the variations sub-group of the chief medical officer's health of the nation working group[70] has recommended that:

- health authorities and GP purchasers should have a plan for identifying and tackling variations [in health], and for evaluating interventions;
- the plan should include provision for working in alliance with other bodies;
- health authorities, GP purchasers and trusts should take steps to monitor access to services to safeguard equitable access;

and that the Department of Health:

- should work actively in alliance with other government departments and other bodies to encourage social policies which promote health;
- should hold the NHS to account for implementation of the recommendations [above]; and
- should take forward recommendations on research.

There is no national strategy for the health of young people. Health promotion policy documents for Wales, Scotland and England in the last decade[43, 71, 72] have made passing reference to special attention being paid to the health needs of young people, as well as socially disadvantaged communities and they have also included health targets for young people.

UK health targets for young people

Achieve a 30% reduction in the number of smokers aged 12–24 (Scotland).

Cut percentage of 15–16 year olds who have ever used drugs to below 10% (Wales).

Reduce the prevalence of regular smoking among 11–15 year olds by at least 33% by 1994 (England).

Reduce the rate of conceptions among the under-16s by at least 50% by the year 2000 (England).

It seems that the scene is set for continuing action to combat variations in health of young people and it can be expected that local, regional and national initiatives will be able to demonstrate some success in helping young people in poverty to aspire to improved health. However, to quote from *The Health Divide*:[73]

> a policy for caring services should be seen as a complement to a wider strategy, rather than a substitute for action on a broader front – nevertheless, there is still a valuable contribution to be made by the health and social services, even though it is recognised that the determinants of health in general, and inequalities in health in particular, mainly lie outside this sector.

Or, as a recent review of interventions for the prevention of suicide worded it:

> to understand the problem of rising suicide in youth, research must address the experience of young men in Britain, and treatment must address aspects of economic and social policy at a national level.[74]

SUMMARY

The main messages in this chapter are:

- there are few high quality research or evaluation studies of interventions to promote the health of young people in poverty;
- statutory and voluntary services have identified the need to work together and to target their action for promoting the health of young people;
- young people must be involved in the design and implementation of initiatives and interventions;
- local community action has potential for success and must be solidly supported by statutory agencies;
- there are clear guidelines for a young people's service at local, regional and national level, and there must be a clear commitment to change from government at these levels; and
- these services for young people can achieve some success but they will be small compared with the effects of alleviating poverty and providing opportunities, particularly that of paid employment.

NOTES

1. L Arblaster et al., Review of the Research on the Effectiveness of Health Service Interventions to Reduce Variations in Health, NHS Centre for Reviews and Dissemination, 1995.
2. L J Gunning-Schepers and A Gepkins, 'Reviews of interventions to reduce social inequalities in health: research and policy implications', Health Education Journal, 1996, 55: 226-38.
3. S Laughlin and D Black, Poverty and Health Tools for Change, Public Health Trust Project, 1995.
4. A Beattie, 'Evaluation in community development for health: an opportunity for dialogue', Health Education Journal, 1995, 54: 465-72.
5. G N Marsh and D M Channing, 'Narrowing the gap between a deprived and an endowed community', British Medical Journal, 1988, 296: 173-6.
6. A Macfarlane, Personal communication, 1996.
7. N Cowap, 'General Practitioners need to be more proactive in providing health care to teenagers', letter to the British Medical Journal, 1996, 313: 941.
8. P Aggleton, G Whitty, A Knight, D Prayle and I Warwick, Management Summary of Promoting Young People's Health, Health Education Authority, 1996.
9. J West, F Hudson, R Levitas and W Guy, Young People and Clinics: Providing for Sexual Health in Avon, University of Bristol, 1995.
10. E C Williams, R J E Kirkman and M Elstein, 'Profile of young people's advice clinic in reproductive health, 1988-93', British Medical Journal, 1994, 309: 786-8.
11. R Playle, J Frankland, V Blakey, C Roberts, L Moore and C Tudor-Smith, The Sexual Health of Young People, Health Promotion, Wales 1995.
12. The Guardian, 25 May 1996.
13. A Kendrick and C Rioch, "Knowing the back roads – rural social work with troubled young people', Youth and Policy, 1995, 57: 46-57.
14. A Graham, L Green and A F Glaster, 'Teenagers' knowledge of emergency contraception: questionnaire survey in south-east Scotland', British Medical Journal, 1996, 312: 1567-9.
15. G Ross, 'Teenage clinics – the rough guide', British Journal of Sexual Medicine, 1996, March/April, 18-22.
16. J Alexander, V Levy and S Rod, Aspects of Midwifery Practice – A Research Based Approach, Macmillan, 1995.
17. K Shanks, BYPASS – The awareness of health, Virtual Image, Dublin, 1995.
18. Health Advisory Service, Children and Young People Substance Misuse Services – the Substance of Young Needs, Health Advisory Service, 1996.

19. Health Advisory Service, *Child and Adolescent Mental Health Services – Together We Stand*, Health Advisory Service, 1995.

20. L Appleby, T Amos, U Doyle, B Tomenson and M Woodman, 'General Practitioners and young suicides – a preventive role for primary care', *British Journal of Psychiatry*, 1996, 168: 330-33.

21. A Cantwell, *Follow the Rough Guide*, National Youth Agenda, 1997.

22. A Macfarlane and A McPherson, 'Primary health care and adolescence', *British Medical Journal*, 1995, 311: 825-6.

23. *Child Protection Messages from Research*, HMSO, 1995.

24. J Gibbons, S Conroy and C Bell, *Operating the Child Protection System: A Study of Child Protection Practices in English Local Authorities*, HMSO, 1995.

25. H Cleaver, *Focus on Teenagers – Research into Practice*, Department of Health, 1996.

26. Barnardo's, *Transition to Adulthood*, Barnardo's, 1996.

27. R Holman, *Putting Families First: Prevention and Child Care: a Study of Prevention by Statutory and Voluntary Agencies*, Macmillan, 1988.

28. L Mitchell, *Smoking Prevention Programmes for Adolescents – a Literature Review*, The National Adolescent & Student Health Unit, Oxford, 1994.

29. D R Gerstein and L W Green, *Preventing Drug Abuse. What do we know?*, National Research Council, 1993.

30. A Oakley, D Fullerton, J Holland *et al.*, 'Sexual health education interventions for young people: a methodological review', *British Medical Journal*, 1995, 310: 158-62.

31. H J Rotheram-Borus, C Koopman, C Haignere and M Davies, 'Reducing HIV sexual risk behaviors among runaway adolescents', *Journal of the American Medical Association*, 1991, 268(9): 1237-41.

32. A R Mellanby, F A Phelps, N J Crichton and J H Tripp, 'School sex education: an experimental programme with educational and medical benefit', *British Medical Journal*, 1995, 311: 414-20.

33. A Seitz and N H Apfel, 'Adolescent mothers and repeated child-bearing: effects of a school-based intervention program', *American Journal of Orthopsychiatry*, 1993, 63: 572-81.

34. H J Walter and R D Vaughan, 'AIDS risk reduction among a multiethnic sample of urban high school students', *Journal of the American Medical Association*, 1993, 270: 725-31.

35. D Nutbeam, P Macaskill, C Smith, J M Simpson and J Catford, 'Evaluation of two school smoking education programmes under normal classroom conditions', *British Medical Journal*, 1993, 306: 102-7.

36. P L Ellickson, R M Bell and M S McGuigan, 'Preventing adolescent drug use: long term results of a junior high program', *American Journal of Public Health*, 1993, 83: 857-61.

37. G J Botvin, E Baker, L Dusenburg, E M Botvin and T Diaz, 'Long-

term follow-up results of a randomised drug abuse prevention trial in a white middle class population', *Journal of the American Medical Asoociation*, 1995, 273: 1106-11.

38. L L Eggert, E A Thompson, J R Herting, L J Nichlas and B G Dicker, 'Preventing adolescent drug abuse and high school dropout through an intensive school based social network development program', *American Journal of Health Promotion*, 1994, 8: 202-15.

39. M H Becker and L A Maiman, 'Socio-behavioural determinants of compliance with health and medical care: recommendations', *Medical Care*, 1980, 13: 10-24.

40. A Bandura, *Social Foundations of Thought and Action: A Social Cognitive Theory*, Prentice-Hall, Englewood Cliffs, New Jersey, 1986.

41. L Azjen and M Fishbein, *Understanding Attitudes and Predicting Social Behaviour*, Prentice-Hall, Englewood Cliffs, New Jersey, 1980.

42. E Rogers, *Diffusion of Innovations*, Free Press, New York, 1983.

43. K Tones and S Tilford, *Health Education: Effectiveness, Efficiency and Equity*, Chapman & Hall, 1994.

44. R Bunton, S Murphy and P Bennett, 'Theories of behavioural change and their use in health promotion: some neglected areas', *Health Education Research*, 1991, 6: 153-62.

45. *Health of the Nation: A Progress Report*, HMSO, 1992.

46. P Bywater and E McLeod (eds), 'Researching women's health work: a study of the lifestyles of mothers on income support', *Working for Equality in Health*, Routledge, 1996.

47. N Melton, G Coldwell and K Peach, *Facilitating, Promoting and Evaluating Peer-led Harm Minimisation Messages*, Lifeline, 1996.

48. *Caring Matters,* Newsletter, Dorset Health Authority, 1996.

49. D L Olds, C R Henderson, R Tatelbaum and R Chamberlain, 'Improving the life course development of socially disadvantaged mothers: a randomised trial of nurse home visitation', *American Journal of Public Health*, 1988, 78: 1436-45.

50. P MacKeith, R Phillipson and A Rowe, *45 Cope Street – Young Mothers Learning through Group Work*, Nottingham Community Health Services, 1991.

51. R Halpern and L Covey, 'Community support for adolescent parents and their children: the parent to parent program in Vermont', *The Journal of Primary Prevention*, 1983, 3: 160-73.

52. Z Johnson, F Howell and B Mellor, 'Community mothers' programme: randomised controlled trial of non-professional intervention in parenting', *British Medical Journal*, 1993, 306: 1449-52.

53. L L Davidson, M S Durkin, L Kuhn, P O'Connor, B Barlow and M C Heagarty, 'The impact of the Safe Kids/Healthy Neighbourhoods Prevention Program in Harlem, 1988 through 1991', *American Journal of Public Health*, 1994, 84: 580-6.

54. C A Johnson, M A Pentz, M D Weber *et al.*, 'Relative effectiveness of comprehensive community programming for drug abuse prevention with high-risk and low-risk adolescents', *Journal of Consulting and Clinical Psychology*, 1990, 58: 447–56.

55. A Ross (unpublished), *Evaluation of the Barri Grubb Food Project*, 1994.

56. *Sexual Health Strategy*, Dorset Health Authority, 1996.

57. *EndHouse, Durham Young People's Centre*, Save the Children, 1996.

58. *Birmingham CAT Adolescent Programme Evaluation*, MORI Health Research Unit, 1995.

59. D Hill, Personal communication, 1992.

60. S Chapman, 'Tobacco control', *British Medical Journal*, 1996; 97: 97–100.

61. J Townsend, P Roderick and J Copper, 'Cigarette smoking by socio-economic group, sex, and effects of price, income, and health policy', *British Medical Journal*, 1994, 309: 923–7.

62. A Marsh and S McKay, *Poor Smokers*, Policy Studies Institute, 1994.

63. D Reid, 'How effective is health education via mass media communications?', *Health Education Journal*, 1996, 5(3): 332–44.

64. M Barnard and A Forsyth, 'The social context of under-age smoking: a qualitative study of cigarette brand preference', *Health Education Journal*, 1996, 55: 175–84.

65. D While, S Kelly, W Huang and A Charlton, 'Cigarette advertising and onset of smoking in children: a questionnaire survey', *British Medical Journal*, 1996, 313: 398–9.

66. *Smoking and the Young*, Royal College of Physicians, 1992.

67. *Enforcing the Law on Tobacco Sales to Children*, Faculty of Public Health Medicine, 1996.

68. S A Glantz, 'Preventing tobacco use – the youth access trap', *American Journal of Public Health*, 1996, 86(2): 156–7.

69. *Young Gods, A Matter of Life and Death: Suicide and Young Men: A Guide for the News Media and Those who Work with Them*, Dorset's Health Promotion Agency, 1996.

70. *Variations in Health – What can the Department of Health do?*, DoH, 1995.

71. Health Education in Scotland, *A National Policy Statement*, The Scottish Home and Health Department, 1991.

72. *Caring for the Future*, Health Promotion Authority for Wales, 1994.

73. M Whitehead, *Inequalities in Health: The Black Report and The Health Divide*, Penguin, 1992.

74. D Gunnell and S Frankel, 'Prevention of suicide: aspirations and evidence', *British Medical Journal*, 1994, 308: 1227–31.

The Government should draw up a co-ordinated and positive programme of action to tackle the problem of youth homelessness and improve the life chances of young people

Credit: Jacky Chapman/Format

4 Social policy – the potential for investing in young people

INTRODUCTION

There is a crying need to improve public and professional understanding of the links between health, education and economic policy and the consequences for everyone of the increasing social and economic exclusion of a substantial proportion of the population.[1]

Reform should not be driven by a desire to control expenditure but by the need to respond to economic and social challenges which face our society today.[2]

The severe exclusion suffered by many young people is not of their own making but has its roots in social and economic policy.[3]

National health policies have failed to incorporate an economic policy to help reduce inequalities in health because of the Government's refusal to recognise the relationship between economics and health. Instead, the Government's economic policies have widened those inequalities.[1]

This chapter covers the need to invest in pre-school and school education to maximise both the optimism of young people and their opportunities; it discusses the need to provide for a higher minimum income for young people and their families; and it identifies measures which will aid the transition to independent living. All of these aspects are seen as crucial to securing better health for young people in poverty.

Each policy area is discussed separately, but it is vital to emphasise the close connections between the different policies. Any truly effective reforms must recognise these links and deal with social policy as a whole, not through a piecemeal approach. It is also important to consider how policy affects young people themselves, both as individuals and within the context of their families.

LAYING THE FOUNDATIONS FOR OPPORTUNITY

> Educational achievement makes an important contribution to class differentials in health, then young people in poor areas may experience a double jeopardy — the benefits of investing in young people throughout childhood becomes apparent, especially in relation to their cognitive and psychosocial well-being.[4]

PRE-SCHOOL INVESTMENT

Denying young children pre-school education is a 'national scandal' because it deprives vulnerable children of '... the right start to their lives'. The effects of pre-school education are '... strongest in those from disadvantaged backgrounds'.[5] Access to nursery education appears to be influenced by both the parents' ability to pay and the area in which they live.[6]

The positive effects of early education are well illustrated by the Perry pre-school study in the USA, where children in poor neighbourhoods were randomly assigned to pre-school nursery care or to no special intervention.[7] The group receiving pre-school education were less likely to be illiterate, less likely to be school drop-outs, and more likely to have gone on to further education at age 19.

In addition, there were follow-up comparisons made at age 27, between the groups who had received the child centred programmes and those who had received no pre-school programme at all. Those who had received the programme were more likely to prosper in material and educational achievements and less likely to be arrested or require social work services. Although there must be caution in interpreting results for a relatively small sample size, these findings should certainly encourage other experiments to be set up along the lines of the High/Scope Perry project (see Figure 4.1) because it appears that an early investment in young people addresses the social and educational factors which we have described as so important for health.

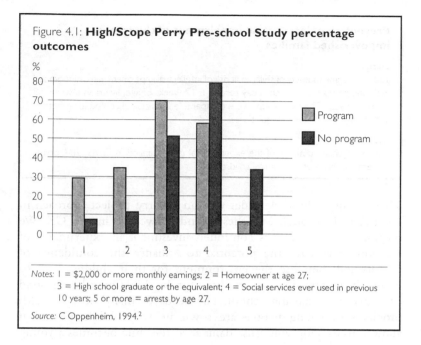

Figure 4.1: **High/Scope Perry Pre-school Study percentage outcomes**

Notes: 1 = $2,000 or more monthly earnings; 2 = Homeowner at age 27; 3 = High school graduate or the equivalent; 4 = Social services ever used in previous 10 years; 5 or more = arrests by age 27.

Source: C Oppenheim, 1994.[2]

Hertzman and Weins have reviewed other pre-school interventions in addition to the Perry project.[8] Examples such as the Parent Child Development Center model, which was applied in three US cities in the 1970s, are discussed. In these programmes service was given to low income populations; primary participants were mothers or other primary caregivers; target age was birth to three years; programmes were of sufficient duration and intensity to maximise their potential effectiveness; and were directed at the full spectrum of problems of poor families by including a broad range of support services. At the age of 3 years, those children in all three cities who had received the programme were more advanced in their development compared with their respective controls.

Another example of pre-school intervention is one from North Carolina, USA.[9]

Prevention of intellectual impairment of children in impoverished families

Design

120 low income mothers of children at risk of intellectual impairment were randomised with one group receiving child day care at 6-12 weeks of age, five days a week, 50 weeks per year. The two groups were comparable for possible confounding factors, such as degree of home stimulation.

Results

The intelligence quotients of the experimental group ranged from 7.9–20.1 points higher than those of the control children.

There is currently work under way on a 'Perry' project approach in Lewisham, Liverpool, Manchester and Newcastle in the UK. We recommend that there is continued investment in experiments of this kind that have the potential to enhance the confidence of parents and therefore the environment for their children, and to ensure the best possible opportunities for the child from a background of deprivation starting school. The seeds of many of the health problems of young people are sown in early childhood and if allowed to develop will cause damage as the child becomes a young person.

KEY RECOMMENDATION

An increase in pre-school investment should be accelerated to lay better foundations for young people.

SCHOOL EDUCATION

There are a number of dimensions to education including preparing young people for other aspects of life, importantly, how to be aware of, and fulfil, their health needs. The Department of Health document *Focus on Teenagers*[10] refers to the importance of education, and health education, in meeting the tripartite needs of young people in relation to health. These needs are:

- the self-confidence to influence their own lives;
- effective coping strategies; and
- prevention through knowledge.

A PORTFOLIO OF SKILLS – EQUAL OPPORTUNITIES FOR ALL?

Schools have a profound influence on the adolescent experience and, it would appear, on their experience of employment, parenthood and social skills.[11]

The portfolio of skills that young people acquire and carry with them throughout their adult life include both the formal and informal aspects of education. Vic Ecclestone, who was made teacher of the year in 1996, refers, in an interview with us, to the latter as 'enrichment skills', and deems them an essential part of the unwritten curriculum. By enabling young people, who might otherwise be denied the opportunity, to participate in a wide range of social and cultural activities, they are able to increase, and enhance, their self-confidence and self-image. School becomes a 'special place' where young people are included in both popular and traditional aspects of the arts. It is particularly important to young people when their creativity is 'taken seriously' and given explicit recognition.

SCHOOL INITIATIVES FOR DEPRIVED YOUNG PEOPLE

In spite of a shortage of resources there are initiatives in schools that are striving to provide the best opportunities for disadvantaged young people.

Carter Community School, Turlin Moor, Bournemouth

This school has 47% slow learners and initiatives include:

- after school homework club;
- sailing club; and
- outward bound course.

Ligoniel School, West Belfast

An after-school study and homework class for traveller children enables them to compete for the 11+ exam.

Bristol Advocacy and Advice Service

The service helps young Black people excluded from school by working with them and with community groups, parents and schools.

KEY RECOMMENDATION

New ideas for improving education services that develop a portfolio of skills for young people should receive special support.

A MARKET OF EDUCATION

There is an increasing reliance on parental contributions and fund-raising for extra curricular activities and necessities. Success in school continues to be seen as the responsibility of the pupil and/or their parents but this does not take into consideration the way in which poor areas have less success in results, not because of so-called 'downward drift' but because there are so many obstacles for young poor people to overcome. Schools are no longer as egalitarian, in theory or in practice, because it is schools rather than young people who are graded and this has created '… a new kind of polarisation between rich and poor'.[12] And it is a polarisation that exists not just between schools but within the school as well, because 'if the economy is believed to be a meritocracy, whatever the human losses the school has to be a meritocracy too'. In class there has to be an underclass and those who are '… unlikely to pass muster are put into the lower streams'. Many young people are only given the chance to fulfil the prophecy of their failure and parents go to extremes in order to get their children into so-called 'good' schools. But this option is not available to young people from poorer households.

New fundraising schemes, such as the recent Specialist School Status (Specialist Schools for Science and Languages, 1994 Education Act, expanded to include Art and Sport in the 1996 Amendment), involve schools raising a minimum of £100,000 from local industry. When this is achieved, the Government matches it and pledges a further £100 per capita payment on each child in the school for the next three years.

The scheme appears quite generous, but there are disadvantages:

- it is not meritocratic because schools do not have to prove excellence in any field, they just have to raise £100,000;
- it is the school's responsibility to attract funding and teachers frequently do this instead of teaching;
- by encouraging industrial funding the state distances itself from responsibility to finance state schools;

- if schools fail to reach the target of £100,000 they do not receive additional funding from the state − even if they achieve say, £80,000 − but they are encouraged to start the process again; and
- in poorer areas there will be less industry to apply to for funding.

So the gap between rich and poor schools becomes wider. The whole area of funding is riddled with anomalies − among many of the LEAs there is little, or no, differentiation in funding school budgets for '... advantaged or disadvantaged areas' within the same authority and the financial autonomy of schools has become increasingly dependent on fund raising by the schools themselves. In the poorest areas any money which is raised pays for 'essentials' such as books rather than for 'extras'.[12]

KEY RECOMMENDATION

There should be a coherent, co-ordinated school funding policy based on the educational needs of young people not on the extent of voluntary funding or partnerships with local industry.

SPECIAL EDUCATIONAL NEEDS

This research reveals the many groups of young people with a multiplicity of needs, who are often overlooked in catch-all policies which are not co-ordinated or constructed to allow for the diverse experiences of young people in contemporary society. The 1988 Education Reform Act and the more recent 1993/4 Special Education Needs (SEN) Code of Practice have encouraged more young people with special needs to be educated in the mainstream sector. However, this has led to an increasing number of young people being recognised as having special needs (intellectual, sensory, emotional or physical) but without a statement to support this. Since local management of schools (LMS) was introduced, schools have become increasingly dependent on local education authorities for SEN funding.

Both the OFSTED report, *Promoting High Achievement for Pupils with Special Educational Needs in Mainstream Schools*,[13] and Teresa Smith and Michael Noble's research[12] refer to the lack of coherence in assessment policies between LEAs. Criteria used to measure young people's needs can vary from area to area and, consequently, the funding varies.[12] This affects the educational opportunities of many young people especially:

- those who are homeless;
- young people from minority ethnic groups who have in the past benefited from Section 11 teachers; and
- disabled young people who want to be included in mainstream education.

The 1996 Ofsted report concludes that one way forward is to stop reducing the number of specialist courses and teachers available while the number of young people with special needs continues to increase. This would go some way towards providing young people with the appropriate services (OFSTED[13] and interview with SEN co-ordinator of one of the largest comprehensives in Avon). As a code of good practice, ATEG, the travellers' education group in Avon, has set up a system where young people are issued with a 'green card' with details of their needs so that they are not denied educational services if and when they move on to another school.

KEY RECOMMENDATION

Young people with special educational needs require a well co-ordinated and resourced service.

GUARANTEEING A MINIMUM INCOME FOR FAMILIES WITH YOUNG PEOPLE

Guaranteeing a reasonable minimum income for young people, through benefits or taxation, can have a direct impact on health, as shown by the results of an experiment in Gary, Indiana, USA, to provide low income young women with a guaranteed income during their pregnancy. The beneficial effects on mother and child were obvious.

Gary income maintenance experiment[14]

Design

Randomised controlled trial using two guaranteed income levels and two tax rates (40% and 60%).

Rationale

Low socioeconomic status is associated with low birth weight; low birth weight is associated with high rates of infant mortality and morbidity; thus, income transfers should increase birth weights in infants born to low income families, and this should have a positive impact on morbidity and mortality both during childhood and later life.

Study group

404 single live births among an urban, Black, low income population in Gary, Indiana. Around one-third of the mothers in the sample were teenagers.

Results

Most of the cohorts whose income was maintained exhibited a beneficial effect on birth weight, particularly those with populations at most risk. This included mothers who both smoke and had a short interval between pregnancies, and mothers under the age of 18 who smoke.

Mothers under 18 showed a greater average response than mothers aged 18–34.

Magnitude of birth weight response did appear to be large enough to constitute a significant health effect.

Beneficial health effect also resulted without provision of direct health services.

The origin of many of the problems we have described lies in the young people and their families struggling to make ends meet and in some cases not having sufficient incentives to be in paid employment.

When proposing changes in socioeconomic policies, it is important to know the cost of living for young people and their families. Research published by CPAG in 1993 showed that the gap between income support rates and a low cost budget was £23 per week for a lone parent with two children, and that for a couple with two children this would be, on average, £45 per week. A recent study analysed the differences in child care costs between different ages and different family structures.[15]

Costs for families of young people

The costs of a child relative to a single adult in one-parent families are substantially higher than in two-parent families (approximately 50% for a child aged 11–18 in a one-parent family compared with under 30% in a two-parent family).

The costs of a child over the age of 11 in one-parent families are significantly higher (at 51% of the cost of a single adult) than that of a child aged under 11 (at 33%).

Older children cost significantly more than younger ones – in a one-parent family with one child, the cost of that one aged 11–18 is about 50% more than that of a child under 11.

The reform of the social security system is often seen as the prime tool in reforming the welfare system. However, it is crucial that any reforms are formulated in the light of changes proposed in other areas such as taxation and employment. It has been argued that growth in social security expenditure is attributable not so much to poor targeting of benefits but to factors on the periphery of the benefit system such as high unemployment and deregulation of the housing market which have contributed to the government's concern over the growth of the public sector borrowing requirement.[2]

Means testing is part of the benefits system and likely to remain so, at least for the near future. However, the substantial disadvantages for young people in poverty should be at the forefront of the agenda for change.

Disadvantages of means-tested benefits include:

- difficult to administer;
- stigma involved in claiming;
- poor take-up;
- disincentive to save;
- relieve rather than prevent poverty;
- create employment disincentive because benefits are withdrawn;
- reduce independence;
- do not provide secure income due to reassessments;
- discourage risk taking in the labour market.

IMPROVEMENTS IN THE SHORT TERM

CPAG would like to see the level of child benefit increased at the very least to compensate for the period covering 1987–1991 when it was frozen. Since 1979 the value of child benefit has fallen by 4 per cent in real terms for the eldest child and 22 per cent for subsequent children. At 1996/97 rates, child benefit would be £11.25 rather than the current level of £10.80 for the first child.

The relationship between child benefit and means-tested benefits is extremely complex and leads to a great deal of confusion. For example, child benefit is taken into account when income support and housing benefit are calculated, but not when family credit is paid out. Furthermore, while child benefit is taken into account as income rather than a cost allowance, it helps to prevent young mothers from falling into unemployment and poverty traps. CPAG would like to see a shift away from means-tested benefits towards child benefit as the main source of income for children and young people and the optimum way to do this for low income families is '... for child benefit to go up each year at a faster rate than the rise in means-tested child allowances'.

Recent proposals have been announced to alter the payment of child allowances in income-related benefits to families with dependants aged 11, 16 and 18 at the times of transition to secondary or further education in order to align with the school year rather than the child's age. Child allowances are supposedly increased in accordance with age to reflect the additional day-to-day expenses and not specifically to meet educational costs at the beginning of the school year. This change is likely to lead to a loss in benefits for some families and may mean some 18 year olds have to leave education.[16, 17] There will be no special rate for 18 year olds and for those on income support or jobseeker's allowance, the changes will mean that families, on average, will be £9.05 a week worse off.[17]

KEY RECOMMENDATION

Reverse recent age-related changes (the '11, 16, 18 clause') in child personal allowances.

The Labour Party is planning to scrap child benefit for 16–18 year olds. They want instead to pay a means-tested top-up allowance for those who stay in full-time education, '... targeted at low and middle income families whose children currently drop out of school' (*Guardian*, 21 September 1996). It will only go to those in '... meaningful education or training' (*ibid*). Labour is also planning to either remove or tax child benefit in wealthier families, although it is yet to commit itself on the definition of 'wealthy' in this context. Although the policy is laudable in trying to target young people from low income families, research by CPAG shows that this policy would risk '... pushing more than 500,000 families into poverty' (*Observer*, 8 September 1996). CPAG is in favour of maintaining the payment as a universal benefit because it is generally well targeted at parents in low and middle income families and take-up is very high. It is doubtful whether low income families would be better off if child benefit were disbanded, as other allowances would simply be recalculated.

KEY RECOMMENDATIONS

Increase child benefit for the first child, at least to make up for the loss from when the benefit was frozen and increase it in future, in line with inflation or earnings (whichever is higher).

Reverse the freeze on the one-parent benefit and lone parent premium.

TAX REFORMS

> The constraints on benefits for unemployed people in the face of a shift in the tax burden in the direction of lower income groups means that the system is less well fitted to cope with poverty among younger people at a time of high long-term unemployment.[18]

Tax reforms have done little to halt the growth in income inequalities. Those paying the top rate of tax have seen their taxation levels fall from 83 per cent to 40 per cent and the basic rate fell from 33 per cent in 1979 to 23 per cent (from April 1997). Reductions in income tax, however, have increased the incomes of those in the highest earnings bracket by a disproportionate amount. Income tax allowances, rather than rates, are much more important to the low paid. Allowances have barely kept up with earnings, while NI contributions and local authority taxes have increased faster than earnings.[19]

Since 1979 those with an income in excess of £80,000 have enjoyed an additional £47,000 per year in tax cuts.[20] At the same time those living on incomes of less than £5,000 received an income tax cut of a mere £140 per year. These meagre gains in income tax for those on low incomes have often been wiped out by increases in other taxes, particularly indirect taxes and reductions in benefit levels and earnings.

Graduated levels of income tax could be introduced so that tax reductions for the poor are paid for by the better off rather than those on middle incomes. This is also preferable from a health point of view as it reduces inequalities in income.[21] The UK is unusual in not having a graduated system (one recommendation is for a graduated income tax structure rising to 50 per cent[22]) and it also has one of the lowest marginal tax rates on high incomes.

KEY RECOMMENDATION

Increase the upper level of tax.

ABOLITION OF NATIONAL INSURANCE CEILING

National insurance contributions are even less progressive than income tax because the upper limit ensures that those with higher earnings pay a smaller proportion of their income in contributions. Those earning £61 a week or less are not entitled to receive any national insurance benefits and, once this threshold is exceeded, NI contributions are payable on all earnings. For young people, the effect of going above the lower earnings limit for insurance contributions is that earners suddenly pay contributions on all their income, not simply on the amount above this limit. This could be avoided through the abolition of the upper limit and converting the lower limit into an allowance.[22]

KEY RECOMMENDATION

Abolish the upper limit for employee national insurance contributions and convert the lower limit into an allowance.

RESTRICTING TAX ALLOWANCES AND RELIEFS

Phasing out tax relief on mortgage interest payments and married couple's allowance would provide savings which could be shifted to the creation of a benefit for low income home owners and improving the level of universal child benefit. Income tax allowances could be converted into a zero rate band.[22] The value of the main personal tax allowance should be restricted to 20 per cent. This is because a higher rate taxpayer saves 40 per cent of the value of the allowance, whereas a standard rate taxpayer saves only 25 per cent of the value of the allowance and a lower rate taxpayer only 20 per cent.

Despite being even more unequally distributed than income, the wealth of the richest is being protected through the reduction in taxes on wealth since 1979.[21] Examples include the reduction in tax liability on capital gains and inheritance tax. The latter is now a flat rate which benefits the largest fortunes. Tax on wealth has not worked particularly well in other countries, where one alternative is a tax on capital transfers.[22]

KEY RECOMMENDATION

Ensure tax allowances do not favour the rich.

INDIRECT TAXATION OF VITAL COMMODITIES SHOULD NOT BE EXTENDED

Indirect taxation should not be seen as a source of funding for child benefit. While the Government has made much of the fact that income taxes have fallen, little is said about the increases in indirect taxation. Indirect taxes take a greater proportion of low income than they do of high income. These increases have shifted the burden of taxation onto middle and lower income groups causing the changes to be a highly regressive form of policy.

KEY RECOMMENDATION

Resist any further increases in indirect taxation of vital commodities and consider reductions in these areas.

LONGER-TERM CHANGES

CPAG has recommended exploration of a family and work model of social security. This model is based on the premise that parents need support both to meet the costs of having children and to maintain the family income through paid work. It also highlights the fact that the social security system should not be considered in isolation from other policies. The key elements of the income aspects of the policy are:

- Social insurance unemployment benefit which is payable on an individual basis.
- Flat rate child benefit payment paid to all families regardless of income.
- A supplement as payment for support with childcare/childrearing costs.

The social insurance unemployment benefit would aim to reduce inequalities between two-earner and no/one-earner families through extending support to individuals who are unemployed but actively seeking work, unable to work because of ill health or are engaged in other activities such as caring. Payment would be made on an individual basis, without dependant additions. In addition to an increase in universal child benefit there would be a childcare/childrearing benefit in recognition of the cost of childcare services or, when a parent chooses to stay at home to look after their young child, in recognition of time costs and loss of income. This payment would need to be paid at a fixed level reflective of actual costs to ensure that it offers a genuine choice to parents, particularly to low income parents.

The barriers to introducing such a model are that such a policy is untested and that it is expensive.[23] As a guide, the gross annual cost of an extra £1 a week universal child benefit for each of 12 million children would be approximately £600m, and a larger increase, together with other benefits for young people, is likely to cost several billion pounds.[5] In effect, funding would have to come from changes in taxation and we see no alternative but for the funds to be found from tax reforms.

KEY RECOMMENDATION

The family and work model should be explored for its potential to benefit the families of young people.

TAX BENEFIT INTEGRATION

Tax benefit integration is aimed at making the system easier for low income families (everybody is assessed once) and to try to get people out of the poverty and unemployment traps. It is also intended to increase co-operation between government and local authority departments so that an increase in one source of income is not compromised by a fall in another. One report argues that a 'strategic integration' may be more feasible than structural integration.[24] This would work by ensuring that the tax and benefit systems work together more effectively, instead of creating poverty and unemployment traps. Any form of tax benefit integration would have to phased in gradually, possibly at higher initial levels for certain groups such as disadvantaged young people[21] or by introducing small transitional new arrangements while gradually replacing other benefits and tax allowances. The system most favoured is a basic income scheme.

BASIC INCOME (BI) SCHEME

BI would pay unconditional benefit to a particular level for every citizen and would be financed by the abolition of tax allowances and some benefits, as well as by higher tax rates for the higher paid. The payment would take the form of a tax credit or allowance, but for those unable to take advantage of it this could be converted into a cash benefit.[21] Alternatively, there is a partial basic income (PBI) whereby people receive less as a tax deduction or a cash credit, but this would then be combined with an income-tested housing benefit and/or a partial negative income tax. The idea behind this is to circumvent the problem of defining how much income is enough to live on, which has to be done when calculating basic income levels.[19]

The main advantages of BI from the viewpoint of young people are:

- strong redistributive effect from paid to unpaid, from rich to poor and across the lifecycle;
- recognition of the growing population of unemployed young people;
- helps to reduce poverty and unemployment traps – a pure BI scheme would eliminate the poverty trap because the marginal tax rate would be similar for everyone until the higher income tax bands are reached and so working is always a financially viable option;[19] and
- provision of a regular income for young people from low income backgrounds – this may be particularly important given that young people sometimes have to wait several weeks for benefits to come through when their situations change.

BI schemes would allow young people the chance to build on the minimum so they can escape poverty more readily in the long term.

These advantages would only come about if a truly common system could be applied for both benefits and taxes. Currently there is a number of obstacles to this, one being that tax is assessed infrequently while benefits for young people are reassessed on a much more regular basis.[24] Further exploration is needed before a basic income model of tax could be contemplated.

KEY RECOMMENDATION

A basic income model of tax benefit integration should be further explored.

AIDING THE TRANSITION TO INDEPENDENCE

One of the key questions for policy makers is the age at which young people should be regarded as adults so that they can gain independent assistance from the state.[3] Young people are treated ambiguously and so the 'dependency assumption' is not applied consistently across the different benefits. While an 18 year old still at school or in 'relevant education' is classed as a child, someone of that age who is unemployed is treated as an adult.

SUPPORT FOR EDUCATION BEYOND 16

In spite of a rise in the last decade of 16–18 year olds staying on in education (from 56 per cent to 69 per cent), over two-thirds of 16 year olds chose to stay in full-time education, but the trend changes with 17, 18 and 19 year olds – 'of OECD countries only Turkey has a lower proportion of 16 and 17 year olds in full-time education'.[25] CPAG has recommended:

- a review of the education/training funding for young people;
- that change in the funding of education/training facilities or for the maintenance of a young person should not jeopardise the opportunities for young people to take up education or training because of their, or their parents', level of income; and
- that changes in the way education maintenance costs are met by the state should not result in families or young people facing a higher risk of falling into poverty.

EDUCATION MAINTENANCE ALLOWANCE

Between 1982 and 1992 the average level of education maintenance allowance (EMA), usually paid direct to the young person, fell by 26 per cent. The level of average allowance varies considerably, from a high of £730 on South Tyneside to £71 in Clwyd. Labour is considering replacing the EMA with an educational allowance paid direct to the parents.[16]

KEY RECOMMENDATION

Education maintenance allowance allocation and payment levels should be made more equitable.

HOUSING BENEFIT

If a young person is paying rent on a property s/he may be entitled to housing benefit. From October 1996, housing benefit payment for under 25s has been restricted to shared accommodation rates. Parents may receive an additional allowance on behalf of the young person who is still living with them as a dependant. If the young person is not a dependant, the parents may face deductions from their housing benefit.

KEY RECOMMENDATION

Housing benefit for young people should be restored to single accommodation rates and reductions against family income should be less punitive.

INCOME SUPPORT/JOBSEEKER'S ALLOWANCE

Entitlement to benefit for many 16–17 years olds was withdrawn in 1988. Under the current rules unemployed 16 and 17 year olds do not receive income support unless they fall into a prescribed category or are in 'severe hardship'. Those applying for 'severe hardship' payments must show that they are available for training as well as work. The number of young people in this age group who are jobless but receive no benefit at all has reached its highest-ever total – 120,300. This has placed an extra burden on the income levels of both young people and their families, many of whom are already on very low incomes. From October 1996, jobseeker's allowance has replaced unemployment benefit and income support for claimants who are unemployed and required to be available for and actively seeking work. As under the previous income support rules, 16 and 17 year olds are not automatically entitled to jobseeker's allowance.[26]

Even for those 16 and 17 year olds who are entitled, the personal allowances are set at a much lower rate than for those aged 18–24. The forerunner to income support, supplementary benefit, had no dividing line related to age. Rather, a higher rate was paid to householders to reflect the higher costs of setting up home as a young person.

New guidelines introduced in summer 1995 tightened up eligibility for severe hardship payments. Those living away from home now need proof from parents or an appropriate third party to prove that they are doing so 'of necessity' because, the Government argues, benefits should be withheld from claimants '... until they provide all the evidence needed to prove their entitlement'.[27] Charities are worried that this will increase homelessness because most young people who live on the streets do not want their parents to know they have been living rough. Roger, a 17 year old, said, after moving to his first hostel in London having run away from home, '... it took two months to convince them [the Department of Social Security] I couldn't get a job, even though I was so young and had no qualifications'.[28] These fears seem to have been partly confirmed by evidence from Youthaid which states that claims for income support fell by approximately 1,000 between summer 1995 and spring 1996.[17] Sixteen and 17 year olds wishing to claim for severe hardship provision can expect to spend three and a half hours in the jobcentre, not including the visit to the careers service which they need to make first.[29]

Income support has '... 100 per cent tax rates' applied to recipients' incomes (including both partners in a couple) beyond a very small weekly 'earnings disregard'.[30] That is to say, benefits are deducted pound for pound as earnings increase and this therefore offers a disincentive for young people to work. There is also the risk of coming off the security of benefit because if, for example, the job fails, then there is the time-consuming process of resuming benefits, with the ensuing delay in receiving income.

Another worry is that those who quit their jobs voluntarily or are dismissed for misconduct are disqualified from receiving unemployment benefit for up to 26 weeks. This is likely to discourage young people from experimenting with jobs that they have not done before or feel they might not be able to handle. Constant contact with the labour market is crucial to getting back to work, as skills need to be maintained and improved, and part-time or temporary jobs might lead to more permanent employment.

Many companies pay out wages one month in arrears which makes the transition from welfare to work extremely difficult for some young people, who will lose their benefits and other entitlements almost as soon as they start work. A large number of young people go into jobs which are low paid, and so will struggle to pay back debts incurred during this transition. As well as the loss in benefits and the lack of publicly subsidised childcare, there are other expenditures such as the purchase of work clothes, travel expenses to and from work, and repayments on loans which may have been provided from the social fund. There is also a sharp increase in housing costs associated with coming off income support, and the move from benefits to work for young lone parents induces higher marginal tax rates due to the combination of means-tested benefit tapers and high work-related costs as already mentioned.[16] The Government has recognised this problem to some extent through the introduction of extended payments (allowing people who move off benefits into work to retain some benefit for the first four weeks) and the back-to-work bonus (which allows claimants to accrue a credit in their earnings while on income support or jobseeker's allowance).

Contribution-based jobseeker's allowance, which replaced unemployment benefit in October 1996, is paid for six months as opposed to 12 months for unemployment benefit. There was a further cut in the level of benefits for young people. While unemployment benefit was paid at the same rate regardless of age, contribution-based jobseeker's allowance is paid at the lower rate for under 25s. The Government assumes that young people continue to have the option of being supported by their parents but the fact remains that 1.16 million 18–24 year olds do not live with family or a partner. CPAG argues that claimants in this category will suffer an annual loss of more than £1,500.[31] Young people in rural areas are likely to be especially affected as all jobseeker's allowance claimants will have to travel to their nearest jobcentre once a fortnight, at their own expense, in order to sign on rather than claiming by post. It is estimated by CPAG that as many as two-thirds of postal claimants could face transport costs of up to £8 per journey.[31] CPAG argues that the new jobseeker's agreement which people must sign as a declaration of their actions in looking for work will make it easier for jobcentre staff to deny benefit if any doubt exists over whether the claimant is genuinely seeking work.[31]

KEY RECOMMENDATIONS

Restore entitlement to benefit for 16–17 year olds on the same basis as older people.

Equalise the benefit rates for the under and over 25s.

Repeal the punitive elements of the jobseeker's allowance.

SOCIAL FUND GRANTS

More payments from the social fund should take the form of grants rather than loans. This would assist young people who are paying off loans from already low weekly benefits, particularly those who are long-term unemployed (previously, donations took the form of grants called single payments). It would also be of great assistance to those who are trying to enter the labour market but have to do so at a wage barely above the benefit level, as well as those who are setting up home. Evidence suggests that grants are more likely to be provided for those on higher equivalent incomes while those on lower incomes are more likely to receive loans. The result has been that '...social fund loan repayments account for a significant part of the fall in the real income of the poorest tenth of the population through the 1980s'.[32] Paradoxically, many of those seeking a loan have been turned away because their incomes are too low to meet the repayments.[33] This will almost certainly lead to a spiralling debt problem and often to less reputable money lenders. Sadly, '... being young and having children significantly increases the risks, with younger and larger families having more debts than older and smaller families'.[33]

KEY RECOMMENDATIONS

Restore the social fund to a grant system.

Restore entitlement to benefit for 16–17 year olds on the same basis as older people.

Equalise the benefit rates for the under and over 25s.

Repeal the punitive elements of the jobseeker's allowance.

BENEFITS FOR DISABLED YOUNG PEOPLE

It is very difficult to assess the true cost of caring and being cared for. Both carer and dependant may experience: loss of independence, career, pension and privacy, a below average income and often an erosion of other aspects of a relationship, love and affection perhaps, and a loss of differentiation between what has been referred to as 'caring for' and 'caring about'.[34] Care, particularly for young people, needs to be provided as a continuum which does not deteriorate as needs change — especially during the period of transition into adulthood.[35-37] But provision of care is often constrained by lack of financial resources and dependency on benefits.

Long-term dependence on benefits, especially for young disabled people who leave school and have no opportunity to enter the labour market, often means that they have far less control over their income (that is, usually benefits) and far less disposable income than their able-bodied peers.

Disempowerment of young disabled people

Many young people have little or no control over their benefits.

Some are unaware of how much their benefit payments amount to.

Young people are not always aware of what benefits are being claimed on their behalf.

Being given 'adult' status by social security when they are 16 does not mean that they become financially independent. This independence often has to be negotiated with parents/carers.

In some instances parents may have become dependent on their children's benefits/allowances.

The point here is not that parents are living from their disabled children's income, but that the costs of disability are in so many ways incalculable. For example, young people with disability may be seen as being a 'burden on their family' which does not mean that families do not want to care but that for many young people there will be no transition from care to independence and this, realistically, is financially constraining because benefits allow for few extras, luxuries or special one-off purchases.[35, 36] The main anxiety of parents with children who are severely disabled is a financial one and how, when their daughter/son is 'looked after in a way that would satisfy them, a great load would be lifted from them'.[38] Disabled young people in minority ethnic families may be particularly disadvantaged.

> There are large numbers of Black disabled people who require health and social services, although they may not be easily identifiable in population surveys.[39]

> There is a very low take-up of means-tested benefits amongst ethnic minority families due to: lack of knowledge, lack of access to services due to institutional racism and the imposition of perceived needs by service providers.[40, 41]

A recent report shows how difficult it can be for young people with disabilities to be independent from their carers and to participate in sport and leisure activities because of financial constraints and lack of transport. They recommend that 'anything that can be done in order to aid this process should be welcomed'. Adults with disability interviewed about their experiences as disabled young people said that they had only qualified for benefits if they fulfilled the stereotype of a helpless disabled person and one man was asked why he tried, or wanted to work at all. Day centres, used as an alternative to employment, were seen as symbolising permanent unemployment and as a way of marginalising issues surrounding disability.[42]

KEY RECOMMENDATION

There should be a sensitive approach to the benefit needs of disabled young people.

IMPROVED CHILDCARE PROVISION FOR YOUNG MOTHERS

A recent study found the key factor affecting lone mothers' employment in the UK is the very high level of childcare costs.[43] This is compounded by the relatively sharp increases in housing costs in the UK when young people come off income support. Improvements in provision would greatly assist the flexibility in the type of job they could apply for. Under family credit, which provides extra income for parents on low wages, childcare costs of £60 are taken into account as an 'income disregard'. However, this allowance only applies to care provided by registered nurseries or childminders and so the scheme is irrelevant to many families who use informal carers. Also, this is the maximum amount paid each week regardless of the number of children needing childcare.[19] Professional childcare is expensive, with the average fee per month for a childminder being £346.[43] In most other industrialised nations, childcare is either free or very heavily subsidised.

KEY RECOMMENDATION

Review the opportunities to subsidise child day care for young parents.

MATERNITY BENEFITS

Young women aged between 16 and 17 are not eligible for income support until the last 11 weeks of their pregnancy.

Income support for 16 and 17 year olds before the last eleven weeks of pregnancy is only paid when the claimant can prove 'unavoidable severe hardship'.

Income support levels for women under 25 do not allow for an adequate expenditure on food for a pregnant woman.

An adequate diet for a 'healthy' expectant mother would cost approximately 50% of the income support (IS) allowance for a single, pregnant woman aged 18–24 and 65% for a 16–17 year old.

A free pint of milk a day and vitamin supplements A, C and D are available for young pregnant women only when they have qualified for IS.

£100 one-off maternity payment for young people is only available if savings are less than £500.[44]

The arbitrary cut-off age of 24 for lower benefit payments, especially to young women who are pregnant, is quite inexplicable when looked at in the context of the needs of a pregnant 24 year old and those of a 25 year old – they are identical. But one vital difference is that the same nutritional requirements would use 49 per cent of the younger woman's income and 39 per cent of the 25 year old's. For younger women of 16 and 17 who do not live in the parental home a basic diet to meet their nutritional needs could cost in excess of 50 per cent of their income. The reasoning behind these differential benefit levels is that it is assumed that young people are more likely to be receiving support from friends and family and that they have fewer responsibilities. But the all party committee commented that making such assumptions about very young mothers '... is putting such mothers and babies at further unnecessary risk'. Young mothers often have to contend with their unborn child's growth and their own nutritional requirements as adolescents.

It is necessary to increase the social fund maternity payment to a level which more closely reflects the cost of caring for a new born child.

KEY RECOMMENDATION

Redesign and improve the maternity benefits paid to young mothers.

EMPLOYMENT

The stance on macroeconomic policy since 1979 is that unemployment is a necessary consequence in the fight against inflation. However, many of the young unemployed are effectively outside the labour market and so have no influence on the process of wage determination. It is highly unlikely that increases in the pay of the young unemployed population are going to fuel inflationary pressures to any serious degree. Policies to help young people need to be seen from the macro as well as the micro point of view. Indeed, '... the forces at work range from international competitiveness and changes in the global labour market to the difficulties faced by young people growing up on high unemployment council estates. As a corollary, policy responses confined to one or two narrow areas are unlikely to be adequate.'[30]

MEASURES TO REDUCE DIFFERENTIALS IN EARNINGS

Even for those fortunate enough to find employment, both wages and job security are very low. It has been estimated that '... roughly 96 per cent of all young people under 18 are on low pay (as defined by the Council of Europe's 'decency threshold' of 68 per cent of all full-timers' mean earnings).[45] The under 18s are the only group of wage earners whose average weekly wage fell between 1992 and 1995.[46] Wages before tax dropped by nearly 1 per cent for young men to £112.80, and by nearly 6 per cent for women to £103.30.

Those from Black minority groups are disproportionately represented in low paid occupations and in sections of the economy where there is a lack of job security, few employment rights and high rates of unemployment.[32] Unemployment rates for Black people and other ethnic minority groups are '… roughly twice those of white people and Black and ethnic minority employees are more likely to be low paid'.[25]

The wage differential between those who leave school with good grades and go on to university, and those who leave school with poor grades, is growing.[30] It is not just that young people are being paid less than their predecessors in real terms, but also that '… their prospects of increasing real earnings with age look bleak'.[30]

KEY RECOMMENDATION

Take action to reduce inequitable differentials in earnings for young people and consider a minimum wage level for young people.

EMPLOYMENT SUPPORT FOR YOUNG PEOPLE LEAVING CARE

Research carried out in Strathclyde stresses the consequences for the employment prospects of young people aged 11 and over who have been in long-term care and have suffered a disrupted education as a result.[47] The young people who were interviewed were often critical of mainstream education provision and were particularly concerned that support would stop at 16. They stressed the need for continuing social work support to help them in their quest for employment. The unemployment rate for care leavers aged 16–19 years is more than twice the national average at around 50 per cent.[10] The majority leave care in poverty. The lower income support rate for 18–24 year olds is based on the assumption that young people of this age remain in households with other adult members but for most young people leaving care, this is not the case.

KEY RECOMMENDATION

Special support should be available for steering young care leavers into further education/training/employment.

SUBSIDIES FOR EMPLOYERS TO TAKE ON THE LONG-TERM UNEMPLOYED YOUNG PERSON

Long-term investment by employers in the training and education of young people should be actively encouraged. Employers often have disincentives to train due to poaching by competitors or uncertain returns on investment.[48, 49] It is Labour's intention to raise around £3 billion from a windfall tax on the privatised utilities and to use it to pay employers a bonus to take on the long-term unemployed.[50]

KEY RECOMMENDATION

Increase employers' subsidy to take on unemployed young people.

RELAXATION OF THE RULE LIMITING EDUCATION TO NO MORE THAN 16 HOURS PER WEEK FOR THE UNEMPLOYED

> Government policy is to encourage people into colleges but to deprive them of benefit should they try to study full-time.[46]

The acquisition of new skills is often vital for those who have been out of the labour market for a significant period of time. Those attending part-time courses have to prove they are still looking for work and have to be willing to leave the course as soon as a suitable vacancy becomes available. Young people whose low academic achievements make them less employable are thus being deterred from improving themselves by the vagaries of the benefit system.

KEY RECOMMENDATION

**Allow young people to claim benefit while studying
more than 16 hours per week.**

IMPROVEMENTS TO YOUTH TRAINING SCHEMES

I'm not really bothered about working. It's not worth it. I've been
on schemes, but they just pay £10 more than the dole. And the
wages round here are so low you're better off with the dole.

Ann, an 18 year old from Sunderland.[51]

The post–school experiences of young people remain strongly
influenced by social class background.[52]

I started on a YT course but couldn't manage on £29.50 a week and
couldn't cope with all the responsibilites so I left the course. Then
my benefits stopped while things were being 'sorted out'. I had no
money and got into trouble with the landlord, so left the flat. I slept
on a friend's floor for a while but there wasn't any room so I went to
an advice agency who referred me to a homeless hostel.[53]

I got £40 for a 40-hour week. They was meant to train you, but all I
did was sweep the floor unless it was busy.

17 year old studying hairdressing
on a youth training programme.[46]

If you go on placement you do the same as an ordinary man, but they
are on £180 and you're only getting £35 a week.

17 year old male in Sunderland talking of his experience on a
bricklaying placement.[48]

If they cannot be part of that system for whatever reason, then it's
awful to say it, but that is not my responsibility.

A representative of a Training and Enterprise Council in
Sunderland talking about young people.[48]

A lot of the ones who remain on the waiting list are people with
special needs.

Report from a London Training Enterprise Council.[54]

Three-quarters of all job training received by school leavers at 16 is
funded under youth training (YT) programmes which were introduced in 1991 to replace the youth training scheme (see Table 4.1).

In April 1996, 260,000 young people were on YT programmes.[17] A further 27,200 participants are on modern apprenticeships which began in April 1995.

TABLE 4.1: **Numbers of young people entering youth training**

	1990/91	1991/92	1992/93	1993/94	1994/95
Young people	347,800	290,400	286,700	290,300	303,600

Source: House of Commons, *Hansard*, 11 July 1996, col. 305.

There are not enough places to meet demand, largely due to the lack of grants which have been eroded by years of spending cuts in local authorities. The image and status of YT schemes needs to be improved to attract more young people into structured programmes and the range of occupational YT areas needs to be expanded. The Labour Party would like to abolish Youth Training programmes as they now stand. Youthaid and the Unemployment Unit welcome Labour's 'Target 2000' proposals in terms of its commitment to making youth unemployment its highest priority but one aspect which is of concern is the element of 'compulsion' in the 'new deal' which states that '... every 16–24 year old will have access to education and training (either full- or part-time) and every young person will achieve National Vocational Qualification (NVQ) level 2 in skills by the age of 18'.[55] Currently only 64 per cent of young people reach level 2 by the age of 19. Concern is also raised that guaranteed access will render a safety net unnecessary, especially as there is no mention of restoring benefits for 16 and 17 year olds who are seeking but have yet to find work or training. Instead, it is argued that '... restoration of a benefit safety net is crucial in order to break the link between income entitlement and the delivery of training, a link which has damaged both the economic welfare of 16–17 year olds and the quality of their training'.[55]

Youthaid critique of YT programmes[52]

One in three young people fails to achieve NVQ level 2.

Barely half gain any qualification of credit towards NVQ.

Half leave early.

About 40% of leavers become unemployed.

Clear differences exist between schemes offered by different employers and sponsors.[56] Employer led programmes, although variable in quality, are recognised by young people as offering the best chance of decent training and a job at the end, whereas programmes run by local authorities or charities and based in workshops or training centres are the least successful in placing trainees in permanent employment – these are also the programmes that often cater for the least qualified or the most vulnerable,[56] and young people who are least likely to get a training place when places are scarce, particularly as some Training and Enterprise Council (TEC) funding for training schemes is linked to the qualifications gained by the trainees.

Youth trainees also tend to be clustered, most prominently by gender, in a limited number of occupational areas. These tend to be clerical, cleaning, catering or selling jobs for females, while male areas are more diverse but tend to be clustered in construction, mining and manufacturing.[56] Training places often do not reflect the occupational areas where most jobs are available, nor the skill levels most in demand. Young men, in particular, need to be more flexible in today's labour market as deindustrialisation and labour market deregulation has led to a more part-time, service sector ethos as opposed to the more traditional jobs that young men used to take up.

An organisation called 'Street CRED'[48] carried out research on some of the most deprived estates in Sunderland where only 8 per cent of young people get jobs when they leave school. Youth unemployment accounts for almost one-third of total unemployment in the area. Only 11 per cent are on Youth Training programmes – at the expense of NVQs.

Street CRED findings

One in eight had no contact with Careers Advisory Service. Two-thirds of those interviewed were neither working, on a training programme, nor in education. These young people are thus already outside the system.

Young people wanted real training and real jobs, for real reward, at the end of the programme. Training is often confused with labouring. Differences in wages should only be permitted when there is an explicit training element and a genuine chance of a job at the end.

Nearly all the respondents complained that they were doing similar work to others but only getting a small proportion of their pay. A common phrase was 'slave labour'. Payment has been frozen at £29.50 per week for 16 year olds since 1989

continued opposite ...

continued ...

and £35 per week for 17 year olds since 1986. If payments had risen in line with average earnings, they would now be worth £76.53.[16] Some pressure groups have recommended an increase to a minimum of £50 per week in order to attract young people into training and allow them to meet basic needs.[16]

Many feel they are forced into YT programmes that they don't want to do, particularly as lack of benefits means that some of them are under pressure from family to go out and bring some money in. Young people want more choice of YT programmes, with a genuine guarantee of places for everyone.

One-third of those who went on post-YT training (employment training, employment action, or training for work) felt they received no training in the job they wanted. Around two-thirds of those who started on one of these programmes did not complete the course. Around 80% who went on a programme felt it didn't help them get a job. Few of them are even familiar with the latter two schemes. More flexibility is needed in the transition between YT and post-YT schemes, and then the transition to work.

The former community programme should have been maintained together with a compulsory element of training because young people received a year's contract together with real work and real pay. However, the government disbanded it due to the high costs in terms of initial outlay, despite the obvious potential for long-term savings.

Young people with special needs should be more closely catered for. General NVQs are often more useful for these people but funds are being squeezed.

There are some good training schemes for young people, and a few examples follow.

Team Wearside

Design

Team Wearside is funded by the local TEC and supported by a number of local employers. It enables 40 very disadvantaged young people each year to benefit from training. One of its major supporters is Vaux Breweries, a major employer on Wearside and provider of many YT placements. Youth trainees are taken on specifically to train them for work, with around 70% continuing with the company at the end of the training period.

Results

This project is seen to be effective at dealing with people with special needs, particularly those who have been severely abused or involved in crime from an early age. Often, it is not deemed to be cost effective for employers to undertake what is often very basic training, so that these people are often '...forced through a qualification system which does not meet their abilities and needs'.[44] Basic life and work skills are taught and work placements are initially offered for three months to familiarise them with the world of work. The success rate is very promising. Of the last 25 leavers from the scheme, 20 have stayed on as employees with the employer who had worked with them.

Learning to care

A Barnardo's /Merseyside TEC project providing opportunities for 16–18 year olds to gain quality training, experience and National Vocational Qualifications while working with children with learning difficulties.

The centre provides courses lasting up to two years and training involves placement in a hospital or school chosen by the young person. Many of the young people initially lack confidence and have low self-esteem. Staff work with individuals and small groups to help boost written and verbal communication skills and improve confidence generally. The project actively seeks to provide equal opportunities, for example seeking placements in Black communities and ensuring that a wide range of issues are covered in the training programme.

The chance to work project

Barnardo's, Merseyside TEC and Social Services Department project to support young people who have learning difficulties and high support needs and help them find a job which meets their requirements.

A relationship is built with a personal job trainer who works with them on a one-to-one basis and accompanies them on work placement. All young people leave with a record of achievement.[57]

Troubleshooter project

Wandsworth Youth Justice has been reported as having a particularly good provision of bail support options for 15 year olds not wishing or unable to continue in education. They have developed a specialist in the careers service to work with young people in trouble with the law. Options available include work shadowing, work experience, early entry to vocational courses and opportunities to develop vocational skills on a project run by the voluntary sector.[58]

One report argues that young people from minority ethnic groups are underrepresented both in employment and on modern apprenticeships even when they have similar qualifications as white people.[59] The report goes on to praise 'positive action' (PA) training initiatives which involve '... empowering people with skills through high quality high incentive training'.[59] It is claimed that a growing majority of employers support the ideals of PA training as a means of combating the lack of experience among ethnic minority job applicants. The success rate for PA schemes is impressive with four in five getting jobs compared with less than one in three for standard youth training programmes. However, PA initiatives are few and far between.

> **KEY RECOMMENDATION**
>
> **Innovative youth training schemes should be used as development models.**

HOUSING

In the absence of adequate accommodation the estimated 150–250,000 homeless young people in Britain find it difficult to maintain a place on a training course or in further education, to access benefits, or to seek and maintain employment. Disabled young people face particular problems from a shortage of suitable housing. Part III of the Housing Act (1985) for England and Wales, Part II of the Housing (Scotland) Act (1987) and Housing (Northern Ireland) Order (1988) all require local councils to give advice and assistance to anyone who is homeless or threatened with homelessness. For those accepted as being homeless, in 'priority need' and unintentionally homeless the local authority has a duty to secure accommodation. Unfortunately, the Housing Act (1985) does not include single people within the definition of 'priority need' unless they are a 'person who is vulnerable as a result of old age, mental illness or handicap, physical disability or other special reason'.

The Homelessness Code of Guidance for Local Authorities (1991) which accompanies the above Housing Acts, advises local authorities to consider the extent to which a young person might be at risk and therefore vulnerable as a result of being homeless. In practice very few local authorities define young people as being vulnerable on the basis of their age alone and so the majority of young people who apply as homeless are found to be ineligible.[57] The 1996 Housing Act removes the duty of local authorities to provide permanent accommodation for 'priority need' homeless people, including those with children. Small wonder that CHAR's 1996 investigation into young people and homelessness, *We don't choose to be homeless*,[60] stresses the need for more coherent policies, greater co-operation between government departments and voluntary agencies and, most importantly, initiatives which prevent homelessness and unemployment.

Wakefield accommodation project

Barnardo's Wakefield Metropolitan District Housing and Social Services Departments provide a service for young people who are homeless or threatened with homelessness. It provides drop-in sessions, a newsletter, individual work and a housing and advice service. There is also a supported lodging scheme with 14 providers, shortstop and night stop provision for assessment or one night stays only and links with the local authority and housing associations to access long-term housing. Young people are helped to plan their future housing and support needs by attending the Children Act Housing Panel where the partnership agencies are all present.[57]

FOYER STYLE PROVISION OF CO-ORDINATED SERVICES FOR YOUNG PEOPLE

The provision of services through Foyers, offering a holistic approach to young people's needs, is strongly recommended. However, as CHAR makes clear, it is necessary to employ an adequate number of professionals in these centres to meet the needs of young people. A large proportion of young people who use the 2,000 bed spaces provided by Foyers lack basic literacy skill and this increases the risk of unemployment, poor housing and ill health.[61]

In short-term emergency accommodation, it is difficult for support workers to provide the level of tuition and supervision many young people need to improve their basic skills. Apart from the Foyers, CHAR does cite other examples of good practice in improving young people's educational skills and employment opportunities. In addition to those young people who become homeless because they have either run away from an unhappy or abusive home, or have been told to leave by family or carers, young people of school age also live in temporary bed and breakfast accommodation with their parent(s) as part of a homeless household. These young people have particular needs because:

- they often have to change school if their temporary housing is in another area;
- young people in temporary accommodation are frequently labelled as a 'problem' or 'low achiever';
- temporary accommodation '… often lacked basic facilities such as chairs and tables as well as offering no privacy, making it difficult for older pupils to study or do homework'.[62]

Homelessness is often assumed to be an urban problem but because young people in rural areas may not have access to services such as young people's centres, their housing needs may be overlooked. Young people often migrate to urban areas because there is no housing, affordable or otherwise, for young single people in rural areas. In 1996, there was an attempt to set up a Foyer project, providing short-term supportive housing and employment/education/training initiatives in response to local need in Shropshire and Herefordshire. However, local residents did not want homeless young people coming to the area. They are, according to one resident, '... reluctant to share their idyll with others less privileged'.[63] This demonstrates the extent to which homelessness carries with it the stigma and the overriding assumption that young people do not belong in rural areas.

Young people who are homeless are also denied their right to participate in bringing about change as citizens – by voting. Again, there does not appear to be any consistent nation-wide policy on registering transient or homeless people to vote, and both CHAR and *The Big Issue* are campaigning for homeless people to be included on the electoral register.

> Not only are homeless people denied a roof over their heads but they are denied civil and political rights ... The right to vote is fundamental in every society.
>
> John Wadham of *Liberty*[64]

Even when young people are provided with housing of some form they have the additional problems of finding furniture, deposits for utilities and buying basic foods. CHAR (1994) recommends the introduction of 'a setting up home grant' which does not have to be repaid. Repayment loans do not relieve poverty, they foster it. The implicit assumption in social policy that all young people have family networks to support them through the transition to independent living is, we would argue, fallacious. As shown in Chapters 1 and 2, neither the changing composition of the family nor the changing nature of work is reflected in welfare reforms or social policy legislation.

A Barnardo's report on young people who have left care has recommended a range of long-term, short-term, semi-supported and independent options and a choice of alternative accommodation.

> **Housing provision required for young people at risk**
>
> - emergency direct access accommodation for crisis situations;
> - supported hostels;
> - supported lodgings;
> - lodgings with former foster parents;
> - Foyers;
> - self-build housing;
> - private rented, furnished and unfurnished accommodation;
> - local authority and housing association tenancies;
> - access to independent housing advice; and
> - option to defer the option of a secure tenancy to age 25.[53]

KEY RECOMMENDATION

The Government should draw up a co-ordinated and positive programme of action to tackle the problem of youth homelessness and improve the life chances of young people.

SUMMARY

The main messages in this chapter are:

- an increase in pre-school investment is needed and new ideas are required for improving education services that develop a portfolio of skills;
- young people with special educational needs require a well co-ordinated and resourced service;
- increase child benefit and strengthen the single parent premium with extra support for the first child;
- reverse the 11, 16, 18 clause in child personal allowances;
- increase the upper level of tax, abolish the upper limit for employee national insurance contributions and convert the lower limit into an allowance and ensure tax allowances do not favour the rich;
- resist any further increases in indirect taxation of vital commodities and consider reductions in these areas;
- explore the family and work model and basic income tax models;
- education maintenance allowance allocation and payment levels should be made more equitable;
- housing benefit for young people should be restored to single

accommodation rates and reductions against income should be less punitive;

- restore income support for 16–17 year olds, the social fund to a grant system employment benefit of at least 12 months, repeal the punitive elements of the jobseeker's allowance system and promote a sensitive approach to the benefit needs of disabled young people;
- review the opportunities to subsidise child day care for young parents and redesign the maternity benefits paid to young mothers;
- take action to reduce inequitable differentials in earnings for young people and provide special support for steering young care leavers into further education/training/employment;
- increase employers' subsidy to take on unemployed young people and allow young people more than 16 hours per week education without benefit penalty;
- innovative youth training schemes should be used as development models; and
- the Government should draw up a co-ordinated and positive programme of action to tackle the problem of youth homelessness and improve the life chances of young people.

NOTES

1. G C M Watt, 'All together now: why social deprivation matters to everyone', *British Medical Journal*, 1996, 312: 1026-9.
2. C Oppenheim, *The Welfare State: Putting the Record Straight*, CPAG, 1994.
3. N Harris, 'Youth, citizenship and welfare', *Journal of Social Welfare and Family Law*, 1992, 175-92.
4. P Johnson and H Reed, *Two Nations? The Inheritance of Poverty and Affluence*, Institute for Fiscal Studies, 1996.
5. F Bennett, *Social Insurance. Reform or Abolition?*, Institute for Public Policy Research, 1993.
6. D Macleod and S Beavis, 'Britain trails rivals for want of skills', *Guardian Education*, 14 June 1996.
7. L J Schweitzer, H V Barnes and D P Weikart, *Significant Benefits: The High/Scope Perry Preschool Study through Age 27*, High/Scope Press, Ypsilanti, Michigan, 1993.
8. C Hertzman and M Weins, 'Child development and long-term outcomes: a population health perspective and summary of successful interventions', *Social Science and Medicine*, 1996, 43: 1083-95.
9. S L Martin, C T Ramey and S Ramey, 'The prevention of intellectual impairment in children of impoverished families', *American Journal of Public Health*, 1990, 80: 844-7.

10. Department of Health, *Focus on Teenagers: Research into Practice,* HMSO, 1996.
11. A Macfarlane *et al., Health of the Young Nation: Synopses of Main Presentations & Personal Profiles,* Report 3 July 1995.
12. T Smith and M Noble, *Education Divides,* CPAG, 1995.
13. OFSTED, *Promoting High Achievement for Pupils with Special Educational Needs in Mainstream Schools,* 1996.
14. B H Kehrer and C M Wolin, 'Impact of income maintenance on low birth weight: evidence from the Gary Experiment, *Journal of Human Resources,* 1979, 14: 434–62.
15. Joseph Rowntree Foundation, *The Cost of Children and the Welfare State,* Social Policy Research 89, December 1994.
16. L Harker, *Could Do Better: Young People, Education and Training,* CPAG, 1996.
17. B Chatrik and P Convery, '120,000 young unemployed people have no income', *Working Brief,* Youthaid, 1996, 77: 15–17.
18. V George and P Taylor-Gooby, *European Welfare Policy,* Macmillan, 1996.
19. H Parker, *Taxes, Benefits and Family Life,* Institute of Economic Affairs, 1995.
20. C Pond, 'Across the great divide', *New Statesman and Society,* 14 October 1994, 28–9.
21. A Quick and R Wilkinson, *Income and Health,* Socialist Health Association, 1991.
22. J Hills, *Changing Tax: How the Tax System Works and How to Change It,* CPAG, 1989.
23. L Harker, *A Secure Future,* CPAG, 1992.
24. D Clinton, M Yates and D Kang, *Integrating Taxes and Benefits?,* Institute for Public Policy Research, 1994.
25. L Harker, 'Poverty of action', *Community Care,* 29 August–4 September 1996, 1–8.
26. Richard Poynter, *Jobseeker's Allowance Handbook,* CPAG, 1996.
27. Peter Lilley, in the *Guardian,* 24 July 1996.
28. The *Guardian,* 24 September 1996.
29. I Maclagan, 'How many unemployed? A surprising new figure for joblessness', *Working Brief,* Youthaid, 1996: 78.
30. Joseph Rowntree Foundation, *Inquiry into Income and Wealth,* Volume 1, 1995.
31. Child Poverty Action Group, *'Policing' Unemployed People,* CPAG, 1996.
32. H Graham, 'The changing financial circumstances of households with children', *Children and Society,* 1994, 8: 98–113.
33. I Maclagan, *Guide to Training and Benefits for Young People,* Youthaid, 1996.

34. J Finch and D Groves, *Community Care the Family: A Case for Equal Opportunties: Woman and Social Policy*, Macmillan, 1985.

35. D Harker, Effect of community care policies and the importance of transition planning for each young person, Telephone conversation, 28 August, 1996.

36. P Alcock, 'Disability and poverty', *Understanding Poverty*, 1993, 174-89.

37. G Dalley, *Ideologies of Caring*, Macmillan, 1990.

38. A Richardson and J Ritchie, *Making the Break*, Kings Fund, 1986.

39. N Begum, *Beyond Samosas and Reggae: a Guide to Developing Services for Black Disabled People*, Kings's Fund, 1995.

40. W I U Ahmad and T A Sheldon, 'Race and statistics' in *Social Research, Philosophy, Politics and Practice*, Radical Statistics, 1993.

41. Y Gunaratnam, *Call for Care*, Kings Fund, 1991.

42. J Preece, 'Class and disability: influences on learning expectations', in *Disability and Society*, 1996, 11: 191-204.

43. Joseph Rowntree Foundation, *Lone Mothers and Work*, Social Policy Research Findings, 1996.

44. NCHMA, *Poor Expectations*, NCH Action for Children and The Maternity Alliance, 1995.

45. V Kumar, *Poverty and Inequality in the UK – The Effects on Children*, National Children's Bureau, 1993.

46. M Hill and J Aldgate, *Child Welfare Services: Developments in Law, Policy, Practice and Research*, Jessica Kingsley Publishers Ltd, 1996.

47. P Gregg, 'Why job creation alone will not solve unemployment' in *Jobs and Justice*, Institute for Public Policy Research, 1993.

48. C Wilkinson, *The Drop Out Society: Young People on the Margin*, Youth Work Press, 1995.

49. *Daily Express*, 1 October 1996.

50. *Observer*, 23 July 1995.

51. *Observer*, 15 September 1996.

52. J Pilcher and H Williamson, *A Guide to Young People's Experience in a Changing Labour Market*, Youthaid, 1987.

53. Barnardo's, *Too Much Too Young: The Failure of Social Policy in Meeting the Needs of Care Leavers*, Barnardo's, 1996.

54. I Maclagan, *Broken Promise: The Failure of Youth Training Policy*, Youthaid and The Children's Society, 1992.

55. 'Labour's New Deal for the under 25s', Working Brief, Youthaid, 1996, 75.

56. B Coles, *Youth and Social Policy*, UCL Press Limited, 1995.

57. Barnardo's, *Transition to Adulthood*, Barnardo's, 1996.

58. The Howard League, *Troubleshooters: A Project to Rescue 15 Year Olds from Prison*, The Howard League, 1995.

59. D Shire, 'Mandela visit shows up apartheid in UK employment'

Working Brief, Youthaid, 1996, 75.

60. CHAR, *We don't choose to be homeless,* CHAR, 1996. (Report of the National Inquiry into preventing youth homelessness.)

61. M Young and A H Halsey, *Family and Community Socialism,* Institute for Public Policy Research, 1995.

62. E Malos, *You've Got No Life: Homelessness and the Use of Bed and Breakfast Hotels,* University of Bristol, 1993.

63. The *Guardian,* 6 October 1996.

64. P N Young, 'Homeless being denied the right to vote', *Young People Now,* February 1996 (Editorial).

Young women living in short-term accommodation provided by Homeless Action. Combined with other provision, this type of housing is essential for meeting the needs of young people.

Credit: Brenda Prince/Format

A study in England and Wales concluded that more comprehensive intervention than school health education alone will be needed to reduce smoking

Credit: Brenda Prince/Format

5 A plan to improve young people's health

INTRODUCTION

In this final chapter, stock is taken of the key messages and recommendations are given, with attention paid to how these can be translated into action. A framework for action is proposed, with consideration of how leadership for action can best be provided at local, regional and national level. Finally a statement of purpose and an action plan is recommended.

KEY MESSAGES AND RECOMMENDATIONS

The key messages and recommendations are summarised as problems and solutions, as follows:

Problems	Solutions
stereotypes	responsible media
low sense of wellbeing	community support
poverty	benefits and tax redistribution
lack of early education	pre-school investment
alienation from school	re-establish pastoral care
inadequate training	monitor and give resource incentives
no job	job placement
no house	create a range of local housing options
minority ethnic groups, disabled, in care	targeted help
advertising	regulation
accidents	community action
respiratory illness and mental ill health	GP recognition and treatment
sexual risks and substance misuse	young people's advisory centres with outreach

In Chapter 1 the stereotyping of young people was described. The irony of these stereotypes is that they give prominence to young people but convey unrealistic and inappropriate images.

Poverty is a term that is unfashionable among politicians. We have not attempted to debate different definitions of poverty here, but simply to reflect many young people's experiences. Since they cannot aspire to the kind of life portrayed in the media and by targeted advertising, a sense of deprivation is engendered. With this comes a lack of optimism, hope, aspirations and a low sense of wellbeing. This becomes an underlying basis of poor health in young people which carries over to their future adult lives. Poverty has a continuing effect on health throughout the life course; from conception, through childhood and adolescence, and into adult life.

It is made clear in Chapter 2 that poverty is associated with five main areas of ill health: accidents, respiratory illness, mental ill health, sexual health and substance misuse. In Chapter 3 it was explained that it is difficult to evaluate interventions by randomised controlled trial and that other forms of rigorous evaluation should be undertaken. Successful interventions include GP services, outreach, young person advisory centres, providing a continuing adult mentor and champion, providing 'Healthy Alliances' of services within community initiatives, peer support for young parents, and doctor advocacy. All local initiatives require positive media support and government action against the promotion and sale of unhealthy products to young people. An agenda for health, health education, social and voluntary services action is proposed, requiring a policy and organisational framework to redirect service effort into real healthy alliances. We make it clear that this type of innovative action will be seriously limited in its efforts to improve the health of young people unless there is also major social policy change.

In Chapter 4 we proposed many key recommendations for social policy change, some with significant resource implications. Is there any chance of these being translated into action? The current political debate is dominated by politicians' fear of alienating the middle classes who they believe want reduced taxes and selective education. At the same time there is apparent concern with personal morality, but not, it seems, with the public immorality of a widening poverty divide. Poverty is a term rarely heard on the lips of policy makers, even though 1996 was the International Year for the Eradication of Poverty. The Government has so far refused to honour its commitment, made at the United Nations Social Summit, to draw up a poverty eradication plan. There is a far greater focus on issues such as benefit fraud, which perpetuate the view that people in poverty are scroungers or petty criminals. This shifts attention away from the need for government action to support individuals, typified by the move to introduce a 'Beat a Cheat' hotline barely a month after closing down the Benefits Advice line. On the plus side, economic prospects are improving, although there is great uncertainty about the effects of eventual entry into European monetary unity.[1]

A FRAMEWORK FOR ACTION

Policies and legislation in the many different sectors that have an impact on young people's health-education, employment, social services, youth, culture and sport-as well as health care are rarely co-ordinated in such a way as to provide a systematic approach to young people's health.[2]

In 1986 the First International Conference on Health Promotion in Ottawa led to the declaration of the Ottawa Charter, which states that if we are to promote health we must:

- build healthy public policy;
- create supportive environments for change;
- strengthen community action;
- develop personal skills; and
- reorient the health service.

There is no need to invent a charter for young people, but there is a need to apply the Ottawa Charter to young people in poverty. This would widen the narrow lens of the 'Health of the Nation' and should incorporate a 'bottom up' approach that is truly informed by the views of young people.

BUILD HEALTHY PUBLIC POLICY

To create a policy for a healthy public we need:

- a national strategy and plan;
- regulation of unhealthy products and marketing;
- media guidelines;
- intersectoral collaboration;
- involvement of young people;

- development of services for deprived young people;
- improved benefits;
- improvements in education;
- improvements in training;
- more job opportunities; and
- improved housing.

CREATE SUPPORTIVE ENVIRONMENTS

The creation of supportive environments requires:

- urban and rural planning;
- transport services;
- targeted help; and
- young people's advisory centres.

STRENGTHEN COMMUNITY ACTION

In order to strengthen community action there has to be:

- commitment from statutory authorities;
- sound resourcing; and
- media support.

DEVELOP PERSONAL SKILLS

The development of personal skills requires:

- user friendly schools;
- training schemes;
- continuing education for young people; and
- disabilities support.

REORIENTATION OF THE HEALTH SERVICES

In order to reorientate the health services there must be:

- improved general practice service for deprived young people;
- improved collection of data on young people's health;
- improved research into young people's health;
- training of health workers on special needs of young people;
- improved mental health services for young people; and
- improved services for young drug misusers.

LOCAL ACTION

In our view it is imperative that one agency is given the lead to promote the health of young people so that there is co-ordinated local action accountable to central government. There are three services that might be considered the main candidates to lead action to promote the health of young people: the youth services, social services and the health service. The choice of lead service will depend on central government's faith in the ability of an organisation to carry responsibility in a way that does not conflict with central policy. Some possible options for choice of lead service are considered below.

THE YOUTH SERVICE

Historically the youth service, as part of the education service, has never been a priority for local authorities and its development has been seriously constrained by lack of resources. The Thompson Report, which reviewed the service in 1982,[3] identified as major issues: concerns about the training of youth workers, staff development, partnership with the voluntary sector and a gap in grounded theory for the development of youth work practice. By the end of the 1980s the youth service was being asked to be more accountable for the funding it received and to voice more articulately its aims, objectives and indicators of its success. It was not given any role in relation to new developments, such as youth training schemes. Conferences in 1989/90 produced a Statement of Purpose for the Youth Service which was considered too radical for the Government. It stated:

> The purpose of youth work is to redress all forms of inequality, to ensure equality of opportunity for all young people to fulfil their potential as empowered individuals and members of groups and communities, and to support young people during the transition to adulthood.

The Minister for Education had asked the youth service conference whether the service should concentrate on 'those who are failed by other services and systems, who are prevented in some way from benefiting from them or simply can't afford them'. The service recommended that its main purpose be to redress the balance and to promote equality of opportunity through challenging oppressions such as racism and sexism.

In 1996, two major reports have urged youth services to target their resources towards disadvantaged and at risk young people.[4,5] Youth services say that they already do this but their resources have been progressively diminished at a time when public demand for their services is at its highest.[6]

SOCIAL SERVICES

In many ways social services are the obvious candidate to be the lead agency for promoting the health of young people. They have a knowledge of the social circumstances that affect the health of young people. They also have the statutory framework of the Children Act. Holman has provided an ambitious list of categories of social work prevention for young people:

- the prevention of removal from their families and received into care;
- the prevention of entry into custodial care;
- the prevention of neglect and abuse of young people;
- the prevention of the effects on young people of poor parenting;
- the prevention of disadvantages associated with the lack of income, amenities and social experiences;
- the prevention of young people staying in care; and
- the prevention of the isolation of young people in care.[7]

In contrast, Pinker, in a review of social workers' roles and tasks, advocated that social workers limit their practice to 'task-centred, problem solving, crisis intervention and behaviour modification methods' as a way of targeting services. Practice 'ought to be preventive with respect to the needs which come to its attention but it has neither the capacity, the resources nor the mandate to start searching for needs in the community at large'.[8]

Pinker's view would appear to have the support of national government which constrained its own Children Act by failing to identify additional resources, and using vague language within the Act such as 'as they consider appropriate' and 'shall take reasonable steps'. Guidance from the DoH in 1992 stipulated that local authority social services departments must measure the resources available to them before making an assessment of local needs in planning for services. Similarly, more recent Acts such as the Health and Community Care Act (1990) and the Carers Act (1995) have reinforced the reality that young persons' needs may not be recognised by social workers if local authorities cannot afford to meet them and that some form of registration such as child protection risk or disability may be necessary to qualify for services.

The Children Act 1989 provided a clear remit for social work services to provide for young people in need, and their families, in particular Section 17 of the Children Act 1989, which 'gives local authorities a general duty to safeguard and promote the welfare of children in need and to promote the upbringing of such children by their families, so far as this is consistent with their welfare duty to the child, by providing an appropriate range of services.' In addition, there is a specific duty on social service authorities to take steps to reduce the need for care or supervision orders and criminal proceedings against young people. The ways in which local authorities interpret the category of children in need is likely to be influenced by financial as well as professional considerations and the tendency has been for child protection issues to dominate the work agenda and deployment of resources. This has meant a concentration on services for young people, for whom the authorities already have responsibility. This is illustrated in the distribution of referrals to social services departments which receive a high priority (see Figure 5.1). In a survey of 82 social services departments, more thn 30 per cent of departments gave a high priority to children at risk of neglect, abuse, those with disability, or those who had offended. On the other hand, only 6 per cent of departments rated poor housing as a priority.[7]

Apart from the apparent lack of involvement of many social services departments with some of the social problems which are strongly related to poor health in young people there are some other formidable obstacles to their being given the lead role for a young people's service. These are:

- the dilution of local government responsibilities;
- reorganisation chaos of local government; and
- reluctance of local voters to pay more for local government services.

These obstacles also apply to the youth service.

There is to be a national review of social services in 1997 and it is to be hoped that these issues will then be addressed.

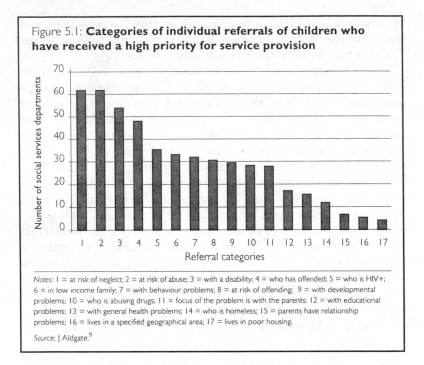

Figure 5.1: **Categories of individual referrals of children who have received a high priority for service provision**

Notes: 1 = at risk of neglect; 2 = at risk of abuse; 3 = with a disability; 4 = who has offended; 5 = who is HIV+; 6 = in low income family; 7 = with behaviour problems; 8 = at risk of offending; 9 = with developmental problems; 10 = who is abusing drugs; 11 = focus of the problem is with the parents; 12 = with educational problems; 13 = with general health problems; 14 = who is homeless; 15 = parents have relationship problems; 16 = lives in a specified geographical area; 17 = lives in poor housing.

Source: J Aldgate.[9]

THE HEALTH SERVICE

The National Health Service, while subject to speculation about the degree to which privatisation will proceed, is actually more secure and better funded than social services. For this reason alone it may be that it should be given the lead role for developing services to promote the health of young people.

Two influential reports by the Health Advisory Service, *Together we stand*, covering the child and adolescent mental health services, and *Substance misuse services – the substance of young needs*, covering drug use and misuse in young people, are stimulating interest in the health service role for improving the problems of disadvantaged and disturbed young people.[10, 11]

> Society's wishes to control those behaviours of young people who are defined as threatening can be more influential than narrow health concerns in defining policy action ... sexual behaviour and illicit use of drugs are examples where social control has clearly been an important consideration.[2]

It has been suggested that the multi-sectoral public policy approach taken to drugs, published in *Tackling Drugs Together*,[12] should be considered as a model for constructing a new public policy framework which would promote young people's health at national, regional and local level. The main elements of this approach are:

- to recognise that there is a problem to be tackled – that of young people in poverty;
- to define the national strategy to tackle that problem;
- to identify the key elements of action to deliver the strategy;
- to monitor progress; and
- to co-ordinate action between departments at national and local level.

This model of developing services for young people's health would require that chief executives of local health authorities are given the responsibility for setting up young people's health action teams. Central funds should be provided for developments and each service represented on the team would be accountable through its own management line for deploying its resources and co-operating with other agencies. Young people would be part of the team. This model should be acceptable to the various agencies.[6]

NATIONAL ACTION

Current government arrangements provide no mechanism by which the needs and interests of young people can be identified – still less protected – when legislative or administrative action by different departments is proposed. The formal links between departments having responsibilities for issues which directly affect young people are limited; interdepartmental consultation is perceived to be grossly inadequate; ministerial leadership is missing and joint action is virtually non-existent.[13]

At national level there must be a central unit for young people's health. There have been proposals regarding the establishment of a Ministry for Youth. Such a ministry would have the role of co-ordination and of assessing the impact on young people's welfare of other large and powerful ministries of state. It is not envisaged that a Ministry for Young People would be an executive agency but rather that it would oversee the development of a more holistic and co-ordinated approach to policy development and may also provide a vehicle through which non-governmental agencies dealing with young people (and including young people themselves) might share in the development of youth policy.

A Statement of Purpose is required for the Ministry for Young People and its plan of action and a suggestion follows.

A government Statement of Purpose for services to improve the health of young people

To take action by vigorous provision of a national system of education and training, welfare benefits, housing provision and social and health care for young people in need in order to:

- prevent young people believing that they cannot be a success;
- reduce ill health in young people and in their subsequent adult lives; and
- prevent premature and tragic early deaths in young people.

Government should monitor the strategy to meet the 'Statement of Purpose' at three levels:

- through a selection of key indicators related to the Statement of Purpose;
- through a system of detailed performance indicators related to the objectives and tasks which flow from the Statement of Purpose; and
- through the periodic review of national and local action to improve services for the health of young people.

A PLAN TO IMPROVE YOUNG PEOPLE'S HEALTH

Based on our review of the evidence, we present suggestions for action to improve the health and wellbeing of young people.

Objective	Action
Raise the national profile of action for young people	Identify a Minister for Young People Launch a national strategy
Improve the media representations aimed at young people	National review of media representations of young people
Reduce unhealthy advertising	Ban cigarette advertising and review situation re other unhealthy products
Raise the local profile of action for young people	Set up local young people's action teams
Increase the voice of young people	Reinforce a national network of young people's representatives
Improve family and young people's benefits	Upgrade child benefit
Improve pre-school education	Introduce a new resource package to stimulate pre-school expansion
Improve training schemes	Take action to remove inequities in training schemes
Take an initiative on young people's housing	Provide increased support for Foyers housing/employment development
Improve transport for young people	Identify and promote good transport models for young people
Raise the profile of community initiatives	Publish results from nationally funded schemes for young people
Develop school initiatives for greater involvement of young people	Identify and promote excellent examples
Services for mental health and drugs misuse	Publish progress report on HAS Reports and 'Tackling Drugs'
Health Service Research and Development programme for young people	Fund further research into young people's health, evaluation of young people's views of services and impact of action on young people's health

In the Appendix, some sources of information are given for those responsible for developing this plan.

THE HEALTH AND WELLBEING OF YOUNG PEOPLE: THE BOTTOM LINE

In this concluding chapter we have summarised material from the rest of the book and ended with some specific recommendations for improving the health and wellbeing of young people. It is important, however, not to forget that the major determinants of progress for young people – and particularly for young people in poverty – are the social investments and economic wherewithal which are available to them. Therefore we conclude this book with a graphic example of how the increasing inequities in British society are contributing to the worsening situation of young people. In Table 5.1 changes in income inequality and changes in the percentage of young people living in poverty are presented for the countries contributing to the Luxembourg Income Study.[14, 15] As can be seen the UK has had the largest change in income inequality, and the largest increase of children living in poverty, of all the countries. This is not a record which should engender pride in any government – rather, it is one which needs to be urgently addressed in the very near future.

TABLE 5.1 **Changes in income inequality and child poverty rate (1967-1992)**

Country	% increase in inequality	% increase in child poverty
UK	more than 30	more than 30
USA	16-29	more than 30
Sweden	16-29	*
Australia	10-15	0
Denmark	10-15	*
Norway	5-10	10-15
The Netherlands	5-10	5-10
Belgium	5-10	5-10
West Germany	0	5-10
Israel	0	5-10
Spain	0	0
France	0	0
Finland	0	*
Canada	0	*
Italy	*	*

Note: * = decrease of at least 5%.
Source: [14, 15]

NOTES

1. *A Budget for the Millennium, Child Poverty Action Group's Budget Briefing*, CPAG, 1996.
2. S Tilford, in J C Coleman and C Warren-Adamson (eds), *Youth Policy in the 1990s: The Way Forward*, Routledge, 1992.
3. *Experience and Participation: Report of the Review Group on the Youth Service in England*, HMSO, 1982.
4. *Misspent Youth*, The Audit Commission, 1996.
5. *The Youth Action Scheme: National Evaluation*, National Youth Agency, Leicester, 1996.
6. B Palmer, Personal communication, 1997.
7. R Holman, *Putting Families First: Prevention and Child Care: A Study of Prevention by Statutory and Voluntary Agencies*, Macmillan, 1988.
8. R Pinker in *Social Workers: Their Roles and Tasks*, National Institute of Social Work, Bedford Square Press, 1982.
9. J Aldgate, *Making Sense of Section 17*, HMSO, 1995.
10. Health Advisory Service, *Child and Adolescent Mental Health Services – Together We Stand*, HMSO, 1995.
11. Health Advisory Service, *Children and Young People Substance Misuse Services – The Substance of Young Needs*, HMSO, 1996.
12. *Tackling Drugs Together*, HMSO, 1994.
13. *'Agenda for a Generation' – Building Effective Youth Work*, United Kingdom Youth Work Alliance, 1996.
14. T M Smeeding and P Gottschalk, 'The international evidence on income distribution in modern economies: where do we stand?', in M Kaiser and Y Mundlak (eds), *Contemporary Economic Development Reviewed*, Vol. 2, Oxford University Press, 1996.
15. J W Lynch and G A Kaplan, 'Understanding how inequality in the distribution of income affects health', *Journal of Health Psychology*, 1997. [In press]

SOURCES OF HELP FOR A YOUNG PEOPLE'S HEALTH PLAN

National Youth Agency (NYA)

17–23 Albion Street,
Leicester LE1 6GD
Tel/Minicom 01533 471200,
Fax 01533 471043

The NYA provides information and support for all those concerned with the informal and social education of young people.

Young People's Health Network

Health Education Authority,
Hamilton House, Mabledon
Place, London WC1H 9TX
Tel 0171 383 3833,
Fax 0171 387 0550

The Action on Aftercare Consortium

First Key, London Office,
London Voluntary Sector
Resource Centre, 365 Holloway
Road, London N7 6PA

National Lottery Charities Board

Tel 01345 919191

Details of funding opportunities.

Barclay's New Futures

Tel 0171 221 7883

Cash awards to help local community initiatives.

Presentation Education and Employment Charitable Trust

Contact: 11–12 Lion Yard,
Tremadox Road,
London SW4 7NQ

A new charity to help Black young people who have been excluded from school.

Directory of Grant Making Trusts: Children and Youth

The directory costs £19.95 from Biblios, Star Road, Partridge Green, West Sussex RH13 8LD, Tel 01403 710851

Youthstart

Contact: Employment Support Unit, ECOTEC, Research and Consulting Ltd, Priestley House, 28–24 Albert Street, Birmingham B4 7UD
Tel 0121 616 3671/3661

This is a programme funded through the European Union for innovative projects to help disadvantaged young people. Services applying must fund 55 per cent of project costs. Priority is given to projects costing in excess of £50,000 per annum.